THE
PROVINCETOWN PLAYS

EDITED AND SELECTED BY
GEORGE CRAM COOK
and
FRANK SHAY

WITH A FOREWORD BY
HUTCHINS HAPGOOD

CINCINNATI
STEWART KIDD COMPANY
PUBLISHERS

5251

Recat. 11-16-48 ee

INTRODUCTION

As these little plays go to press, the news comes of the death of John Reed, of the original group who formed the Players seven or eight summers ago at Provincetown.

Reed was a pure spirit, held completely by what his imagination saw. He acted without reserve and had no prudence. His life was determined by real values. With a gay smile he gave himself to what he saw as beautiful, no matter where it might lead—to ostracism, to prison, to death. He did not express himself solemnly, but he lived a life of passionate devotion to the best, as he saw it.

Reed joins in death several others of the Players who went before; all, but one, young, like him; all, like him, devoted, and careless of the world, careful of the spirit—so reckless and unafraid. "Hutch" Collins, who challenged life at every moment; Pendleton King; Fenimore Merrill; Nani Bailey, who loved all but herself; Alice Macdougall, and the beautiful Mary Pyne, who quietly understood all that youth and age know, and Mrs. E. E. Cook, the oldest member of the Players, but young in spirit.

Youth and death are close companions. United, they are of the eternal. As age comes, youth and death are separated. Only while they are united is art there. Those who were close to the Provincetown Players know how youth was there; and

5

now we see better how death was imminent to the necessary carelessness of pure living and doing.

In the plays contained in this volume, and in others not published or published in previous collections, there are touches that, to those of us who can supply from our memories, reveal the spirit of the Players. This is the best that art can do. To all art we must bring something not contained in it, to see it as art. We must see the unattained youthful effort. If there is a glimpse of that, it is all we can hope for in an unrealized world. These ten are not the best plays ever written; but they are written in a pure spirit; they sprang from an attempt made by a group of men and women to express something sincerely, with no regard for fame, money, or power—and whatever they have of value is due to that.

If the Provincetown Players had not been formed, in unusual degree, with the purity of youth and effort, so many of them would not, in all likelihood, in this brief time have died. It was not an accident. They gave themselves unreservedly to life, and it was eternity, rather than death, that took them.

Among those of the Players who remain there are some who remain unwillingly. Whom the gods love die young, and if some of those who remain are loved of the gods, it is because they are already living beyond in spirit, and are held here for the purpose of fulfilling some mundane obligation.   HUTCHINS HAPGOOD.

ACKNOWLEDGMENTS

Grateful acknowledgment for permission to include plays in this volume is made to the following authors and publishers:

To Alice Rostetter, Susan Glaspell, Neith Boyce, Edna St. Vincent Millay, Rita Wellman, the late Pendleton King, James Oppenheim, Floyd Dell, Wilbur Daniel Steele, Eugene G. O'Neill, George Cram Cook, and Hutchins Hapgood.

To Egmont Arens, for *The Widow's Veil, The Angel Intrudes*, and *Night*. Copies of the acting editions of these plays may be had from Mr. Arens.

To Boni & Liveright, Inc., from *Bound East For Cardiff*.

To Small, Maynard & Company, for *Suppressed Desires*.   F. S.

NOTE

CONTENTS

SUPPRESSED DESIRES

A COMEDY IN TWO SCENES

By George Cram Cook and Susan Glaspell

*A period of two weeks is supposed to elapse be-
tween the first and second scenes.*

PERSONS

HENRIETTA BREWSTER
STEPHEN BREWSTER
MABEL

SUPPRESSED DESIRES

SCENE I

A studio apartment in an upper story, Washington Square South. Through an immense north window in the back wall appear tree tops and the upper part of the Washington Arch. Beyond it you look up Fifth Avenue. Near the window is a big table, loaded at one end with serious-looking books and austere scientific periodicals. At the other end are architect's drawings, blue prints, dividing compasses, square, ruler, etc. At the left is a door leading to the rest of the apartment; at the right the outer door. A breakfast table is set for three, but only two are seated at it—Henrietta and Stephen Brewster. As the withdraw *Steve pushes back his coffee* sits dejected.*

HENRIETTA

It isn't the coffee, Steve, dear. The thing the matter with the coffee. There's ing the matter with *you.*

STEVE *(doggedly)*

There may be something the matter w. stomach.

HENRIETTA *(scornfully)*
Your stomach! The trouble is not with your stomach, but in your subconscious mind.

STEVE
Subconscious piffle. *(Takes morning paper and tries to read.)*

HENRIETTA
Steve, you never used to be so disagreeable. You certainly have got some sort of a complex. You're all inhibited. You're no longer open to new ideas. You won't listen to a word about psychoanalysis.

STEVE
A word! I've listened to volumes!

HENRIETTA
You've ceased to be creative in architecture— your work isn't going well. You're not sleeping well—

STEVE
How can I sleep, Henrietta, when you're always waking me up in the night to find out what I'm dreaming?

HENRIETTA
But dreams are so important, Steve. If you'd tell yours to Dr. Russell, he'd find out exactly what's wrong with you.

STEVE
There's nothing wrong with me.

HENRIETTA
You don't even talk as well as you used to.

STEVE
Talk? I can't say a thing without you looking

12

at me in that dark fashion you have when you're on the trail of a complex.

HENRIETTA

This very irritability indicates that you're suffering from some suppressed desire.

STEVE

I'm suffering from a suppressed desire for a little peace.

HENRIETTA

Dr. Russell is doing simply wonderful things with nervous cases. Won't you go to him, Steve?

STEVE *(slamming down his newspaper)*
No, Henrietta, I won't!

HENRIETTA

But, Stephen!—

STEVE

Tst! I hear Mabel coming. Let's not be at each other's throats the first day of her visit. *(He takes out cigarets. Mabel comes in from door left, the side opposite Steve, so that he is facing her. She is wearing a rather fussy negligee in contrast to Henrietta, who wears "radical" clothes. Mabel is what is called plump.)*

MABEL

Good-morning!

HENRIETTA

Oh, here you are, little sister!

STEVE

Good-morning, Mabel! *(Mabel nods to him and turns, her face lighting up, to Henrietta.)*

HENRIETTA

(giving Mabel a hug as she leans against her)

13

It's so good to have you here. I was going to let you sleep, thinking you'd be tired after the long trip. Sit down. There'll be fresh toast in a minute and *(rising)* will you have—

MABEL

Oh, I ought to have told you Henrietta. Don't get anything for me. I'm not eating breakfast.

HENRIETTA *(at first in mere surprise)*

Not eating breakfast? *(She sits down, then leans toward Mabel, who is seated now, and scrutinizes her.)*

STEVE *(half to himself)*

The psychoanalytical look!

HENRIETTA

Mabel, why are you not eating breakfast?

MABEL *(a little startled)*

Why, no particular reason. I just don't care much for breakfast, and they say it keeps down *(a hand on her hip—the gesture of one who is "reducing")* that is, it's a good thing to go without it.

HENRIETTA

Don't you sleep well? Did you sleep well last night?

MABEL

Oh, yes, I slept all right. Yes, I slept fine last night, only *(laughing)* I did have the funniest dream!

STEVE

S-h! S-t!

HENRIETTA *(moving closer)*

And what did you dream, Mabel?

STEVE

Look-a-here, Mabel, I feel it's my duty to put you on. Don't tell Henrietta your dreams. If you do, she'll find out that you have an underground desire to kill your father and marry your mother—

HENRIETTA

Don't be absurd, Stephen Brewster! *(Sweetly to Mabel)* What was your dream, dear?

MABEL *(laughing)*

Well, I dreamed I was a hen.

HENRIETTA

A hen?

MABEL

Yes; and I was pushing along through a crowd as fast as I could, but being a hen I couldn't walk very fast—it was like having a tight skirt, you know; and there was some sort of creature in a blue cap—you know how mixed up dreams are—and it kept shouting after me, "Step, hen! Step, hen!" until I got all excited and just couldn't move at all.

HENRIETTA

(resting chin in palm and peering) You say you became much excited?

MABEL *(laughing)*

Oh, yes; I was in a terrible state.

HENRIETTA

(leaning back, murmurs) This is significant.

STEVE

She dreams she's a hen. She is told to step lively. She becomes violently agitated. What can it mean?

HENRIETTA
(turning impatiently from him) Mabel, do you know anything about psychoanalysis?

MABEL *(feebly)*
Oh—not much. No—I—*(brightening)* It's something about the war isn't it?

STEVE
Not that kind of war.

MABEL *(abashed)*
I thought it might be the name of a new explosive.

STEVE
It *is.*

MABEL
(apologetically to Henrietta, who is frowning) You see, Henrietta, I—we do not live in touch with intellectual things, as you do. Bob being a dentist—somehow our friends—

STEVE *(softly)*
Oh, to be a dentist! *(Goes to window and stands looking out.)*

HENRIETTA
Don't you ever see anything more of that editorial writer—what was his name?

MABEL
Lyman Eggleston?

HENRIETTA
Yes, Eggleston. He was in touch with things. Don't you see him?

MABEL
Yes, I see him once in a while. Bob doesn't like him very well.

HENRIETTA

Your husband does not like Lyman Eggleston?
(*mysteriously*)   Mabel, are you perfectly
happy with your husband?

STEVE (*sharply*)

Oh, come now, Henrietta—that's going a little
strong!

HENRIETTA

Are you perfectly happy with him, Mabel?
(*Steve goes to work-table.*)

MABEL

Why—yes—I guess so.   Why—of course I
am!

HENRIETTA

Are you happy?   Or do you only think you
are?   Or do you only think you *ought* to be?

MABEL

Why, Henrietta, I don't know what you mean!

STEVE

(*seizes stack of books and magazines and
dumps them on the breakfast table*)   This is
what she means, Mabel.   Psychoanalysis.   My
work-table groans with it.   Books by Freud,
the new Messiah; books by Jung, the new St.
Paul; the Psycho-analytical Review—back num-
bers two-fifty per.

MABEL

But what's it all about?

STEVE

All about your subconscious mind and desires
you know not of.   They may be doing you a
great deal of harm.   You may go crazy with
them.   Oh, yes!   People are doing it right and

2

left. Your dreaming you're a hen—*(Shakes his head darkly.)*

HENRIETTA

Any fool can ridicule anything.

MABEL

(hastily, to avert a quarrel) But what do you say it is, Henrietta?

STEVE

(looking at his watch) Oh, if Henrietta's going to start that! *(During Henrietta's next speech settles himself at work-table and sharpens a lead pencil.)*

HENRIETTA

It's like this, Mabel. You want something. You think you can't have it. You think it's wrong. So you try to think you don't want it. Your mind protects you—avoids pain—by refusing to think the forbidden thing. But it's there just the same. It stays there shut up in your unconscious mind, and it festers.

STEVE

Sort of an ingrowing, mental toe-nail.

HENRIETTA

Precisely. The forbidden impulse is there full of energy which has simply got to do something. It breaks into your consciousness in disguise, masks itself in dreams, makes all sorts of trouble. In extreme cases it drives you insane.

MABEL

(with a gesture of horror) Oh!

HENRIETTA *(reassuring)*

But psychoanalysis has found out how to save

18

us from that. It brings into consciousness the suppressed desire that was making all the trouble. Psychoanalysis is simply the latest method of preventing and curing insanity.

STEVE

(from his table) It is also the latest scientific method of separating families.

HENRIETTA *(mildly)*

Families that ought to be separated.

STEVE

The Dwights, for instance. You must have met them, Mabel, when you were here before. Helen was living, apparently, in peace and happiness with good old Joe. Well—she went to this psychoanalyzer—she was "psyched," and biff!—home she comes with an unsuppressed desire to leave her husband. *(He starts work, drawing lines on a drawing board with a T-square.)*

MABEL

How terrible! Yes, I remember Helen Dwight. But—but did she have such a desire?

STEVE

First she'd known of it.

MABEL

And she *left* him?

HENRIETTA *(coolly)*

Yes, she did.

MABEL

Wasn't he good to her?

HENRIETTA

Why, yes; good enough.

19

MABEL

Wasn't he kind to her?

HENRIETTA

Oh, yes—kind to her.

MABEL

And she left her good, kind husband?

HENRIETTA

Oh, Mabel! "Left her good, kind husband!"
How naive—forgive me, dear—but how bour-
geoise you are! She came to know herself.
And she had the courage!

MABEL

I may be very naive and—bourgeoise—but I
don't see the good of a new science that breaks
up homes. (Steve applauds.)

STEVE

In enlightening Mabel, we mustn't neglect to
mention the case of Art Holden's private sec-
retary, Mary Snow, who has just been informed
of her suppressed desire for her employer.

MABEL

Why, I think it is terrible, Henrietta! It would
be better if we didn't know such things about
ourselves.

HENRIETTA

No, Mabel, that is the old way.

MABEL

But—but her employer? Is he married?

STEVE (grunts)

Wife and four children.

MABEL

Well, then, what good does it do the girl to be

told she has a desire for him? There's nothing can be done about it.

HENRIETTA

Old institutions will have to be reshaped so that something can be done in such cases. It happens, Mabel, that this suppressed desire was on the point of landing Mary Snow in the insane asylum. Are you so tightminded that you'd rather have her in the insane asylum than break the conventions?

MABEL

But—but have people always had these awful suppressed desires?

HENRIETTA

Always.

STEVE

But they've just been discovered.

HENRIETTA

The harm they do has just been discovered. And free, sane people must face the fact that they have to be dealt with.

MABEL *(stoutly)*

I don't believe they have them in Chicago.

HENRIETTA

(business of giving Mabel up) People "have them" wherever the living Libido—the center of the soul's energy—is in conflict with petrified moral codes. That means everywhere in civilization. Psychoanalysis—

STEVE

Good God! I've got the roof in the cellar!

HENRIETTA

The roof in the cellar!

21

STEVE

(holding plan at arm's length) That's what psychoanalysis does! ⟨

HENRIETTA

That's what psychoanalysis could *un*-do. Is it any wonder I'm concerned about Steve? He dreamed the other night that the walls of his room melted away and he found himself alone in a forest. Don't you see how significant it is for an architect to have *walls* slip away from him? It symbolizes his loss of grip in his work. There's some suppressed desire—

STEVE

(hurling his ruined plan viciously to the floor) Suppressed hell!

HENRIETTA

You speak more truly than you know. It is through suppressions that hells are formed in us.

MABEL

(looking at Steve, who is tearing his hair) Don't you think it would be a good thing, Henrietta, if we went somewhere else? *(They rise and begin to pick up the dishes. Mabel drops a plate, which breaks. Henrietta draws up short and looks at her—the psychoanalytic look)* I'm sorry, Henrietta.. One of the Spode plates, too. *(Surprised and resentful as Henrietta continues to peer at her)* Don't take it so to heart, Henrietta.

HENRIETTA

I can't help taking it to heart.

MABEL

I'll get you another. *(Pause. More sharply*

as Henrietta does not answer) I said I'll get you another plate, Henrietta.

HENRIETTA
It's not the plate.

MABEL
For heaven's sake, what is it then?

HENRIETTA
It's the significant little false movement that made you drop it.

MABEL
Well, I suppose everyone makes a false movement once in a while.

HENRIETTA
Yes, Mabel, but these false movements all mean something.

MABEL *(about to cry)*
I don't think that's very nice! It was just because I happened to think of that Mabel Snow you were talking about—

HENRIETTA
Mabel Snow!

MABEL
Snow—Snow—well, what was her name, then?

HENRIETTA
Her name is Mary. You substituted *your own* name for hers.

MABEL
Well, *Mary* Snow, then; *Mary Snow.* I never heard her name but once. I don't see anything to make such a fuss about.

HENRIETTA *(gently)*
Mabel, dear, mistakes like that in names—

23

MABEL *(desperately)*
They don't mean something, too, do they?

HENRIETTA *(gently)*
I am sorry, dear, but they do.

MABEL
But I'm always doing that!

HENRIETTA
(after a start of horror) My poor little sister, tell me all about it.

MABEL
About what?

HENRIETTA
About your not being happy. About your longing for another sort of life.

MABEL
But I *don't.*

HENRIETTA
Ah, I understand these things, dear. You feel Bob is limiting you to a life in which you do not feel free—

MABEL
Henrietta! When did I ever say such a thing?

HENRIETTA
You said you are not in touch with things intellectual. You showed your feeling that it is Bob's profession—that has engendered a resentment which has colored your whole life with him.

MABEL
Why—Henrietta!

HENRIETTA
Don't be afraid of me, little sister. There's nothing can shock me or turn me from you. I

24

am not like that. I wanted you to come for this visit because I had a feeling that you needed more from life than you were getting. No one of these things I have seen would excite my suspicion. It's the combination. You don't eat breakfast *(enumerating on her fingers)*; you make false moves; you substitute your own name for the name of another *whose love is misdirected.* You're nervous; you *look* queer; in your eyes there's a frightened look that is most unlike you. And this dream. A *hen.* Come with me this afternoon to Dr. Russell! Your whole life may be at stake, Mabel.

MABEL *(gasping)*
Henrietta, I—you—you always were the smartest in the family, and all that, but—this is terrible! I don't think we *ought* to think such things *(brightening).* Why, I'll tell you why I dreamed I was a hen. It was because last night, telling about that time in Chicago, you said I was as mad as a wet hen.

HENRIETTA *(superior)*
Did you dream you were a *wet* hen?

MABEL
(forced to admit it) No.

HENRIETTA
No. You dreamed you were a *dry* hen. And why, being a hen, were you urged to step?

MABEL
Maybe it's because when I am getting on a street car it always irritates me to have them call "Step lively."

HENRIETTA

No, Mabel, that is only a child's view of it—if you will forgive me. You see merely the elements used in the dream. You do not see into the dream; you do not see its meaning. This dream of the hen—

STEVE

Hen—hen—wet hen—dry hen—mad hen! *(jumps up in a rage)* Let me out of this!

HENRIETTA

(hastily picking up dishes, speaks soothingly) Just a minute, dear, and we'll have things so you can work in quiet. Mabel and I are going to sit in my room. *(She goes out left, carrying dishes.)*

STEVE

(seizing hat and coat from an alcove near the outside door) I'm going to be psychoanalyzed. I'm going now! I'm going straight to that infallible doctor of hers—that priest of this new religion. If he's got honesty enough to tell Henrietta there's nothing the matter with my unconscious mind, perhaps I can be let alone about it, and then I *will* be all right. *(From the door in a low voice)* Don't tell Henrietta I'm going. It might take weeks, and I couldn't stand all the talk. *(He hurries out.)*

HENRIETTA *(returning)*

Where's Steve? Gone? *(with a hopeless gesture)* You see how important he is—how unlike himself! I tell you, Mabel, I'm nearly distracted about Steve.

SUPPRESSED DESIRES

MABEL

I think he's a little distracted, too.

HENRIETTA

Well, if he's gone, you might as well stay here. I have a committee meeting at the book-shop, and will have to leave you to yourself for an hour or two. (*As she puts her hat on, taking it from the alcove where Steve found his, her eye, lighting up almost carnivorously, falls on an enormous volume on the floor beside the work-table. The book has been half hidden by the wastebasket. She picks it up and carries it around the table toward Mabel*) Here, dear, is one of the simplest statements of psychoanalysis. You just read this and then we can talk more intelligently. (*Mabel takes volume and staggers back under its weight to chair rear center. Henrietta goes to outer door, stops and asks abruptly*) How old is Lyman Eggleston?

MABEL (*promptly*)

He isn't forty yet. Why, what made you ask that, Henrietta? (*As she turns her head to look at Henrietta her hands move toward the upper corners of the book balanced on her knees.*)

HENRIETTA

Oh, nothing. Au revoir. (*She goes out. Mabel stares at the ceiling. The book slides to the floor. She starts; looks at the book, then at the broken plate on the table*) The plate! The book! (*She lifts her eyes, leans forward elbow on knee, chin on knuckles and plaintively queries*) Am I unhappy?

[CURTAIN]

27

SCENE II

The stage is as in Scene I, except that the break-fast table has been removed. During the first few minutes the dusk of a winter afternoon deepens. Out of the darkness spring rows of double street-lights, almost meeting in the distance. Henrietta is at the psychoanalytical end of Steve's work-table, surrounded by open books and periodicals, writing. Steve enters briskly.

STEVE
What are you doing, my dear?

HENRIETTA
My paper for the Liberal Club.

STEVE
Your paper on—

HENRIETTA
On a subject which does not have your sympathy.

STEVE
Oh, I'm not sure I'm wholly out of sympathy with psychoanalysis, Henrietta. You worked it so hard. I couldn't even take a bath without it's meaning something.

HENRIETTA *(loftily.)*
I talked it because I knew you needed it.

STEVE
You haven't said much about it these last two

28

weeks. Uh—your faith in it hasn't weakened any?

HENRIETTA

Weakened? It's grown stronger with each new thing I've come to know. And Mabel. She is with Dr. Russell now. Dr. Russell is wonderful! From what Mabel tells me I believe his analysis is going to prove that I was right. To-day I discovered a remarkable confirmation of my theory in the hen dream.

STEVE

What is your theory?

HENRIETTA

Well, you know about Lyman Eggleston. I've wondered about him. I've never seen him, but I know he's less bourgeois than Mabel's other friends—more intellectual—and *(significantly)* she doesn't see much of him because Bob doesn't like him.

STEVE

But what's the confirmation?

HENRIETTA

To-day I noticed the first syllable of his name.

STEVE

Ly?

HENRIETTA

No—egg.

STEVE

Egg?

HENRIETTA *(patiently)*

Mabel dreamed she was a *hen.* *(Steve laughs)* You wouldn't laugh if you knew how important names are in interpreting dreams. Freud is full of just such cases in which a whole hidden complex is revealed by a single significant syllable—like this egg.

STEVE

Doesn't the traditional relation of hen and egg suggest rather a maternal feeling?

HENRIETTA

There is something maternal in Mabel's love, of course; but that's only one element.

STEVE

Well, suppose Mabel hasn't a suppressed desire to be this gentleman's mother, but his beloved! What's to be done about it? What about Bob? Don't you think it's going to be a little rough on him?

HENRIETTA

That can't be helped. Bob, like everyone else, must face the facts of life. If Dr. Russell should arrive independently at this same interpretation, I shall not hesitate to advise Mabel to leave her present husband.

STEVE

Um—um! *(The lights go up on Fifth Avenue. Steve goes to the window and looks out)* How long is it we've lived here, Henrietta?

HENRIETTA

Why, this is the third year, Steve.

STEVE

I—we—one would miss this view if one went away, wouldn't one?

HENRIETTA

How strangely you speak! Oh, Stephen, I *wish* you'd go to Dr. Russell. Don't think my

fears have abated because I've been able to re-
strain myself. I had to go on account of Mabel.
But now, dear—won't you go?

STEVE
I—(*he breaks off, turns on the light, then comes
and sits beside Henrietta*) How long have we
been married, Henrietta?

HENRIETTA
Stephen, I don't understand you! You must
go to Dr. Russell.

STEVE
I have gone.

HENRIETTA
You—what?

STEVE (*jauntily*)
Yes, Henrietta, I've been psyched.

HENRIETTA
You went to Dr. Russell?

STEVE
The same.

HENRIETTA
And what did he say?

STEVE
He said—I —I was a little surprised by what
he said, Henrietta.

HENRIETTA (*breathlessly*)
Of course—one can so seldom anticipate. But
tell me—your dream, Stephen! It means—

STEVE
It means—I was considerably surprised by what
it means.

HENRIETTA
Don't be so exasperating!

STEVE

It means—you really want to know, Henrietta?

HENRIETTA

Stephen, you'll drive me mad!

STEVE

He said—of course he may be wrong in what he said.

HENRIETTA

He *isn't* wrong.   *Tell* me!

STEVE

He said my dream of the walls receding and leaving me alone in a forest indicates a suppressed desire—

HENRIETTA

Yes—yes!

STEVE

To be freed from—

HENRIETTA

Yes—freed from—

STEVE

Marriage.

HENRIETTA

(crumples. Stares) Marriage!

STEVE

He—he may be mistaken, you know.

HENRIETTA

May be mistaken?

STEVE

I—well, of course, I hadn't taken any stock in it myself.   It was only your great confidence—

HENRIETTA

Stephen, are you telling me that Dr. Russell— Dr. A. E. Russell—told you this? *(Steve nods)*

Told you you had a suppressed desire to separate from me?

STEVE

That's what he said.

HENRIETTA

Did he know who you were?

STEVE

Yes.

HENRIETTA

That you were married to me?

STEVE

Yes, he knew that.

HENRIETTA

And he told you to leave me?

STEVE

It seems he must be wrong, Henrietta.

HENRIETTA (*rising*)

And I've sent him more patients! (*Catches herself and resumes coldly*) What reason did he give for this analysis?

STEVE

He says the confining walls are a symbol of my feeling about marriage and that their fading away is a wish-fulfillment.

HENRIETTA (*gulping*)

Well, is it? Do you want our marriage to end?

STEVE

It was a great surprise to me that I did. You see I hadn't known what was in my unconscious mind.

HENRIETTA (*flaming*)

What did you tell Dr. Russell about me to make him think you weren't happy?

8

STEVE

I never told him a thing, Henrietta. He got it all from his confounded clever inferences. I— I tried to refute them, but he said that was only part of my self-protective lying.

HENRIETTA

And that's why you were so—happy—when you came in just now?

STEVE

Why, Henrietta, how can you say such a thing? I was *sad*. Didn't I speak sadly of—of the view? Didn't I ask how long we had been married?

HENRIETTA (*rising*)

Stephen Brewster, have you no sense of the seriousness of this? Dr. Russell doesn't know what our marriage has been. You do. You should have laughed him down. Confined—in life with me? Did you tell him that I believe in freedom?

STEVE

I very emphatically told him that his results were a great surprise to me.

HENRIETTA

But you accepted them.

STEVE

Oh, not at all. I merely couldn't refute his arguments. I'm not a psychologist. I came home to talk it over with you. You being a disciple of psychoanalysis—

HENRIETTA

If you are going, I wish you would go to-night!

STEVE

Oh, my dear! I—surely I couldn't do that! Think of my feelings. And my laundry hasn't come home.

HENRIETTA

I ask you to go to-night. Some women would falter at this, Steve, but I am not such a woman. I leave you free. I do not repudiate psychoanalysis; I say again that it has done great things. It has also made mistakes, of course. But since you accept this analysis—*(She sits down and pretends to begin work)* I have to finish this paper. I wish you would leave me.

STEVE

(scratches his head, goes to the inner door) I'm sorry, Henrietta, about my unconscious mind. *(Alone, Henrietta's face betrays her outraged state of mind—disconcerted, resentful, trying to pull herself together. She attains an air of bravely bearing an outrageous thing. Mabel enters in great excitement.)*

MABEL *(breathless)*

Henrietta, I'm so glad you're here. And alone? *(Looks toward the inner door)* Are you alone, Henrietta?

HENRIETTA

(With reproving dignity) Very much so.

MABEL

(rushing to her) Henrietta, he's found it!

HENRIETTA *(aloof)*

Who has found what?

35

MABEL

Who has found what? Dr. Russell has found my suppressed desire.

HENRIETTA

That is interesting.

MABEL

He finished with me to-day. He got hold of my complex in the most amazing way! But, oh, Henrietta, it is so terrible!

HENRIETTA

Do calm yourself, Mabel. Surely there's no occasion for all this agitation.

MABEL

But there is! And when you think of the lives that are affected—the readjustments that must be made in order to bring the suppressed hell out of me and save me from the insane asylum—

HENRIETTA

The insane asylum!

MABEL

You said that's where these complexes brought people!

HENRIETTA

What did the doctor tell you, Mabel?

MABEL

Oh, I don't know how I can tell you—it is so awful—so unbelievable.

HENRIETTA

I rather have my hand in at hearing the unbelievable.

MABEL

Henrietta, who would ever have thought it? How can it be true? But the doctor is per-

fectly certain that I have a suppressed desire
for—(*Looks at Henrietta, is unable to continue.*)

HENRIETTA

Oh, go on, Mabel. I'm not unprepared for
what you have to say.

MABEL

Not unprepared? You mean you have suspected it?

HENRIETTA

From the first. It's been my theory all along.

MABEL

But, Henrietta, I didn't know myself that I had
this secret desire for Stephen.

HENRIETTA

(*jumps up*) Stephen!

MABEL

My brother-in-law! My own sister's husband!

HENRIETTA

You have a suppressed desire for *Stephen!*

MABEL

Oh, Henrietta, aren't these unconscious selves
terrible? They seem so unlike *us!*

HENRIETTA

What insane thing are you driving at?

MABEL (*blubbering*)

Henrietta, don't you use that word to me.
I don't *want* to go to the insane asylum.

HENRIETTA

What did Dr. Russell say?

MABEL

Well, you see—oh, it's the strangest thing!
But you know the voice in my dream that called

"Step, Hen!" Dr. Russell found out to-day that when I was a little girl I had a story-book in words of one syllable and I read the name Stephen wrong. I used to read it S-t-e-p, step, h-e-n, hen. *(Dramatically)* Step Hen is Stephen. *(Enter Stephen, his head bent over a time-table)* Stephen is Step Hen!

STEVE

I? Step Hen?

MABEL *(triumphantly)*

S-t-e-p, step, H-e-n, hen, Stephen!

HENRIETTA *(exploding)*

Well, what if Stephen is Step Hen? *(Scornfully)* Step Hen! Step Hen! For that ridiculous coincidence—

MABEL

Coincidence! But it's childish to look at the mere elements of a dream. You have to look *into* it—you have to see what it *means!*

HENRIETTA

On account of that trivial, meaningless play on syllables—on that flimsy basis—you are ready —*(Wails)* O-h!

STEVE

What on earth's the matter? What has happened? Suppose I *am* Step Hen? What about it? What does it mean?

MABEL *(crying)*

It means—that I—have a suppressed desire for *you!*

STEVE

For me! The deuce you have? *(Feebly)* What—er—makes you think so?

MABEL

Dr. Russell has worked it out scientifically.

HENRIETTA

Yes. Through the amazing discovery that Step Hen equals Stephen!

MABEL (*tearfully*)

Oh, that isn't all—that isn't near all. Henrietta won't give me a chance to tell it. She'd rather I'd go to the insane asylum than be unconventional.

HENRIETTA

We'll all go there if you can't control yourself. We are still waiting for some rational report.

MABEL

(*drying her eyes*) Oh, there's such a lot about names. (*With some pride*) I don't see how I ever did it. It all works in together. I dreamed I was a hen because that's the first syllable of *Hen*-rietta's name; and when I dreamed I was a hen, I was putting myself in Henrietta's place.

HENRIETTA

With Stephen?

MABEL

With Stephen.

HENRIETTA (*outraged*)

Oh! (*Turns in rage upon Stephen, who is fanning himself with the time-table*) What are you doing with that time-table?

STEVE

Why—I thought—you were so keen to have me go to-night—I thought I'd just take a run up to Canada, and join Billy—a little shooting—but—

MABEL

But there's more about the names.

HENRIETTA

Mabel, have you thought of Bob—dear old Bob—your good, kind husband?

MABEL

Oh, Henrietta, "my good, kind husband!"

HENRIETTA

Think of him, Mabel, out there alone in Chicago, working his head off, fixing people's teeth —for *you!*

MABEL

Yes, but think of the living Libido—in conflict with petrified moral codes! And think of the perfectly wonderful way the names all prove it. Dr. Russell said he's never seen anything more convincing. Just look at Stephen's last name— Brewster. I dream I'm a hen, the name Brewster—you have to say its first letter by itself— and then the hen—that's me—she says to him: "Stephen, Be Rooster!" *(Henrietta and Stephen collapse into the nearest chairs.)*

MABEL

I think it's perfectly wonderful! Why, if it wasn't for psychoanalysis you'd never find out how wonderful your own mind is!

STEVE

(begins to chuckle) Be Rooster, Stephen, Be Rooster!

HENRIETTA

You think it's funny, do you?

STEVE

Well, what's to be done about it? Does Mabel have to go away with me?

HENRIETTA

Do you want Mabel to go away with you?

STEVE

Well, but Mabel herself—her complex—her suppressed desire—

HENRIETTA

(*going to her*) Mabel, are you going to insist on going away with Stephen?

MABEL

I'd rather go with Stephen than go to the insane asylum!

HENRIETTA

For heaven's sake, Mabel, drop that insane asylum! If you *did* have a suppressed desire for Stephen hidden away in you—God knows it isn't hidden now. Dr. Russell has brought it into your consciousness—with a vengeance. That's all that's necessary to break up a complex. Psychoanalysis doesn't say you have to *gratify* every suppressed desire.

STEVE (*softly*)

Unless it's for Lyman Eggleston.

HENRIETTA

(*turning on him*) Well, if it comes to that, Stephen Brewster, I'd like to know why that interpretation of mine isn't as good as this one? Step, Hen!

STEVE

But Be Rooster! (*He pauses, chuckling to*

41

himself) Step-Hen B-rooster. And *He*nrietta.
Pshaw, my dear, Doc Russell's got you beat a
mile! *(He turns away and chuckles)* Be
rooster!

MABEL

What has Lyman Eggleston got to do with it?

STEVE

According to Henrietta, you, the hen, have a
suppressed desire for *Egg*leston, the egg.

MABEL

Henrietta, I think that's indecent of you! He
is bald as an egg and little and fat—the idea of
you thinking such a thing of me!

HENRIETTA

Well, Bob isn't little and bald and fat! Why
don't you stick to your own husband? *(To
Stephen)* What if Dr. Russell's interpretation
has got mine "beat a mile?" *(Resentful look
at him)* It would only mean that Mabel doesn't
want Eggleston and does want you. Does that
mean she has to have you?

MABEL

But you said Mabel Snow——

HENRIETTA

Mary Snow! You're not as much like her as
you think—substituting your name for hers!
The cases are entirely different. Oh, I wouldn't
have *believed* this of you, Mabel. *(Beginning
to cry)* I brought you here for a pleasant visit
—thought you needed brightening up—wanted
to be *nice* to you—and now you—my husband
—you insist—— *(In fumbling her way to her*

42

chair she brushes to the floor some sheets from the psychoanalytical table.)

STEVE

(with solicitude) Careful, dear. Your paper on psychoanalysis! *(Gathers up sheets and offers them to her.)*

HENRIETTA

I don't want my paper on psychoanalysis! I'm sick of psychoanalysis!

STEVE *(eagerly)*

Do you mean that, Henrietta?

HENRIETTA

Why shouldn't I mean it? Look at all I've done for psychoanalysis—and—*(raising a tear-stained face)* what has psychoanalysis done for me?

STEVE

Do you mean, Henrietta, that you're going to stop *talking* psychoanalysis?

HENRIETTA

Why shouldn't I stop talking it? Haven't I seen what it does to people? Mabel has gone crazy about psychoanalysis! *(At the word "crazy," with a moan Mabel sinks to chair and buries her face in her hands.)*

STEVE *(solemnly)*

Do you swear never to wake me up in the night to find out what I'm dreaming?

HENRIETTA

Dream what you please—I don't care what you're dreaming.

43

STEVE

Will you clear off my work-table so the Journal of Morbid Psychology doesn't stare me in the face when I'm trying to plan a house?

HENRIETTA

(pushing a stack of periodicals off the table) I'll *burn* the Journal of Morbid Psychology!

STEVE

My dear Henrietta, if you're going to separate from psychoanalysis, there's no reason why I should separate from *you*. *(They embrace ardently. Mabel lifts her head and looks at them woefully.)*

MABEL

(jumping up and going toward them) But what about me? What am I to do with my suppressed desire?

STEVE

(with one arm still around Henrietta, gives Mabel a brotherly hug) Mabel, you just keep right on suppressing it!

[CURTAIN]

ARIA DA CAPO

A PLAY

By Edna St. Vincent Millay

First printed in "Reedy's Mirror," St. Louis. Application to produce this play should be made to Edna St. Vincent Millay, in care of the Provincetown Players, 133 Macdougal St., New York.

PERSONS

PIERROT
COLUMBINE
COTHURNUS *(masque of tragedy)*
THYRSIS *(shepherd)*
CORYDON *(shepherd)*

ARIA DA CAPO

The curtain rises on a stage set for a Harlequinade, a merry black and white interior. Directly behind the footlights, and running parallel with them, is a long table, covered with a gay black and white cloth, on which is spread a banquet. At the opposite ends of this table, seated on delicate thin-legged chairs with high backs, are Pierrot and Columbine, dressed according to the tradition, excepting that Pierrot is in lilac, and Columbine in pink. They are dining.

COLUMBINE
Pierrot, a macaroon! I cannot *live* without a macaroon!

PIERROT
My only love, you are *so* intense. . . . It is Tuesday, Columbine? I'll kiss you if it's Tuesday.

COLUMBINE
It is Wednesday, if you must know. . . . Is this my artichoke, or yours?

PIERROT
Ah, Columbine, as if it mattered! Wednesday. . . . Will it be Tuesday, then, to-morrow, by any chance?

47

COLUMBINE

To-morrow will be—Pierrot, that isn't funny!

PIERROT

I thought it rather nice. Well, let us drink some wine and lose our heads and love each other.

COLUMBINE

Pierrot, don't you love me now?

PIERROT

La, what a woman! How should I know? Pour me some wine; I'll tell you presently.

COLUMBINE

Pierrot, do you know, I think you drink too much!

PIERROT

Yes, I dare say I do. . . . Or else too little. It used to tell. You see, I am always wanting a little more than what I have—or else a little less. There's something wrong. My dear, how many fingers have you?

COLUMBINE

La, indeed, how should I know? It always takes my one hand to count the other with. It's too confusing. Why?

PIERROT

Why? I am a student, Columbine, and search into all matters.

COLUMBINE

La, indeed? Count them yourself, then!

PIERROT

No. Or, rather, nay. 'Tis of no consequence. . . . I am become a painter, suddenly—and you impress me—Ah, yes!—six orange bull's-

eyes, four green pin-wheels, and one magenta
jelly-roll—the title as follows: *Woman Taking In Cheese From Fire-Escape.*

COLUMBINE

Well, I like that! So that is all I've meant to
you!

PIERROT

Hush! All at once I am become a pianist. I
will image you in sound, . . . on a new
scale . . . without tonality. . . . *Vivace
senza tempo senza tutto.* . . . Title: *Uptown Express at Six O'Clock.* Pour me a drink.

COLUMBINE

Pierrot, you work too hard. You need a rest.
Come on out into the garden, and sing me something sad.

PIERROT

Don't stand so near me! I am become a so-
cialist. I love humanity, but I hate people.
Columbine, put on your mittens, child; your
hands are cold.

COLUMBINE

My hands are *not* cold.

PIERROT

Oh, I am sure they are. And you must have
a shawl to wrap about you, and sit by the fire.

COLUMBINE

Why, I'll do no such thing! I'm hot as a spoon
in a tea-cup!

PIERROT

Columbine, I'm a philanthropist. I know I am,
because I feel so restless. Do not scream, or
it will be the worse for you!

4

COLUMBINE

Pierrot, my vinaigrette! I cannot *live* without my vinaigrette!

PIERROT

My only love, you are *so* fundamental! . . . How would you like to be an actress, Columbine? I am become your manager.

COLUMBINE

Why, Pierrot, *I* can't act.

PIERROT

Can't act! Can't act! La, listen to the woman! What's that to do with the price of furs? You're blonde, are you not? You have no education, have you? Can't act! You underrate yourself, my dear!

COLUMBINE

Yes, I suppose I do.

PIERROT

As for the rest, I'll teach you how to cry, and how to die, and other little tricks; and the house will love you. You'll be a star by five o'clock. . . . That is, if you will let me pay for your apartment.

COLUMBINE

Let you? Well, that's a good one! Ha! Ha; Ha! But why?

PIERROT

But why? Well, as to that, my dear, I cannot say. It's just a matter of form.

COLUMBINE

Pierrot, I'm getting tired of caviar and pea-cocks' livers. Isn't there something else that people eat—some humble vegetable that grows in the ground?

PIERROT

Well, there are mushrooms.

COLUMBINE

Mushrooms! That's so! I had forgotten . . . mushrooms . . . mushrooms. . . . I cannot *live* with. . . . How do you like this gown?

PIERROT

Not much. I'm tired of gowns that have the waist-line about the waist, and the hem around the bottom, and women with their breasts in front of them! *Zut* and *ehé!* Where does one go from here!

COLUMBINE

Here's a persimmon, love. You always liked them.

PIERROT

I am become a critic; there is nothing I can enjoy. . . . However, set it aside; I'll eat it between meals.

COLUMBINE

Pierrot, do you know, sometimes I think you're making fun of me.

PIERROT

My love, by yon black moon, you wrong us both.

COLUMBINE

There isn't a sign of a moon, Pierrot.

PIERROT

Of course not. There never was. "Moon's" just a word to swear by. "Mutton!"—now

there's a thing you can lay the hands on, and
set the tooth in! Listen, Columbine: I always
lied about the moon and you. Food is my only
lust.

COLUMBINE

Well, eat it, then, for heaven's sake, and stop
your silly noise! I haven't heard the clock tick
for an hour.

PIERROT

It's ticking all the same. If you were a fly, you
would be dead by now. And if I were a parrot,
I could be talking for a thousand years! *(En-*
ters Cothurnus.)

PIERROT

Hello, what's this, for God's sake? What's
the matter? Say, whadda you mean? Get off
the stage, my friend, and pinch yourself—you're
walking in your sleep!

COTHURNUS

I never sleep.

PIERROT

Well, anyhow, clear out. You don't belong on
here. Wait for your own scene! Whadda you
think this is—a dress-rehearsal?

COTHURNUS

Sir, I am tired of waiting. I will wait no
longer.

PIERROT

Well, but what are you going to do? The
scene is set for me!

COTHURNUS

True, sir; yet I can play the scene.

PIERROT

Your scene is down for later!

COTHURNUS

That, too, is true, sir; but I play it now.

PIERROT

Oh, very well. Anyway, I am tired of black and white. At least, I think I am. *(Exit Columbine)* Yes, I am sure I am. I know what I'll do! I'll go and strum the moon—that's what I'll do. . . . Unless, perhaps, . . . you never can tell . . . I may be, you know, tired of the moon. Well, anyway, I'll go find Columbine. . . . And when I find her, I will address her thus: *"Ehé Pierrette!"* There's something in that. *(Exit Pierrot.)*

COTHURNUS

You, Thyrsis! Corydon! Where are you?

THYRSIS

Sir, we are in our dressing-room!

COTHURNUS

Come out and do the scene.

CORYDON

You are mocking us! The scene is down for later.

COTHURNUS

That is true; but we will play it now. I am the scene. *(Seats himself on high place in back of stage. Enter Corydon and Thyrsis.)*

CORYDON

Sir, we were counting on this little hour. We said, "Here is an hour, in which to think a mighty thought, and sing a trifling song, and look at nothing." And, behold! the hour, even as we spoke, was over, and the act begun, under our feet!

THYRSIS

Sir, we are not in the fancy to play the play. We had thought to play it later.

CORYDON

Besides, this is the setting for a farce. Our scene requires a wall; we cannot build a wall of tissue-paper!

THYRSIS

We cannot act a tragedy with comic properties!

COTHURNUS

Try it and see. I think you'll find you can. One wall is like another. And regarding the matter of your insufficient wood, the important thing is that you speak the lines, and make the gestures. Wherefore I shall remain throughout, and hold the prompt-book. Are you ready?

CORYDON-THYRSIS *(sorrowfully)*

Sir, we are always ready.

COTHURNUS

Play the play! *(Corydon and Thyrsis move the table and chairs to one side out of the way, and seat themselves in a half-reclining position on the floor, left of the center of the stage, propped up by crepe paper pillows and bolsters, in place of rocks.)*

THYRSIS

How gently in the silence, Corydon, our sheep go up the bank. They crop a grass that's yellow where the sun is out, and black where the clouds drag their shadows. Have you noticed

how steadily, yet with what a slanting eye they
graze?

CORYDON

As if they thought of other things.   What say
you, Thyrsis; do they only question where next
to pull? Or do their far minds draw them thus
vaguely north of west and south of east?

THYRSIS

One cannot say. . . .   The black lamb wears
its burdocks as if they were a garland—have
you noticed? Purple and white—and drink the
bitten grass as if it were a wine.

CORYDON

I've noticed that. What say you, Thyrsis; shall
we make a song about a lamb that thought himself a shepherd?

THYRSIS

Why, yes!—that is, why—no. I have forgotten my line.

COTHURNUS (prompting)

"I know a game worth two of that."

THYRSIS

Oh, yes. . . .   I know a game worth two of
that: Let's gather rocks, and build a wall between us; and say that over there belongs to
me, and over here to you!

CORYDON

Why—very well. And say you may not come
upon my side unless I say you may!

THYRSIS

Nor you on mine! And if you should, 'twould
be the worse for you! (They weave a wall of
colored crepe paper ribbons from the center

55

front to the center back of the stage, fastening the ends to Columbine's chair in front and to Pierrot's chair in the back.)

CORYDON

Now, there's a wall a man may see across, but not attempt to scale.

THYRSIS

An excellent wall.

CORYDON

Come, let us separate, and sit alone a little while, and lay a plot whereby we may outdo each other. *(They seat themselves on opposite sides of the wall.)*

PIERROT

(off stage) Ehé, Pierrette!

COLUMBINE

(off stage) My name is Columbine! Leave me alone!

THYRSIS

(coming up to the wall) Corydon, after all, and in spite of the fact I started it myself, I do not like this so very much. What is the sense of saying I do not want you on my side the wall? It is a silly game. I'd much prefer making the little song you spoke of making, about the lamb, you know, that thought himself a shepherd! What do you say? *(Pause.)*

CORYDON

(at wall) I have forgotten the line.

COTHURNUS *(prompting)*

"How do I know this isn't a trick?"

56

CORYDON

Oh, yes. . . . How do I know this isn't a trick to get upon my land?

THYRSIS

Oh, Corydon, you *know* it's not a trick. I do not like the game, that's all. Come over here, or let me come over there.

CORYDON

It is a clever trick to get upon my land. *(Seats himself as before.)*

THYRSIS

Oh, very well! *(Seats himself . . . as before)* *(To himself)* I think I never knew a sillier game.

CORYDON

(coming to wall) Oh, Thyrsis, just a minute! All the water is on your side the wall, and the sheep are thirsty. I hadn't thought of that.

THYRSIS

Oh, hadn't you?

CORYDON

Why, what do you mean?

THYRSIS

What do I mean? I mean that I can play a game as well as you can. And if the pool is on my side, it's on my side, that's all.

CORYDON

You mean you'd let the sheep go thirsty?

THYRSIS

Well, they're not my sheep. My sheep have water enough.

57

CORYDON

Your sheep! You are mad, to call them yours
—mine—they are all one flock! Thyrsis, you
can't mean to keep the water from them just
because they happened to be grazing over here
instead of over there, when we set the wall up?

THYRSIS

Oh, can't I? Wait and see! And if you try
to lead them over here, you'll wish you hadn't!

CORYDON

I wonder how it happens all the water *is* on
your side. . . . I'll say you had an eye out
for lots of little things, my innocent friend,
when I said, "Let us make a song," and you
said, "I know a game worth two of that!"

COLUMBINE

(off stage) D'you know, I think you must be
getting old, or fat, or something—stupid, anyway! Can't you put on some other kind of
collar?

THYRSIS

You know as well as I do, Corydon, I never
thought of anything of the kind. *Don't* you?

CORYDON

I *do* not.

THYRSIS

Don't you?

CORYDON

Oh, I suppose so. Thyrsis, let's drop this—
what do you say? It's only a game, you know.
. . . We seem to be forgetting it's only a
game . . . a pretty serious game it's getting

58

to be, when one of us is willing to let the sheep
go thirsty, for the sake of it.

THYRSIS

I know it, Corydon. *(They reach out their
arms to each other across the wall.)*

COTHURNUS *(prompting)*
"But how do I know?"

THYRSIS

Oh, yes. . . . But how do I know this isn't
a trick to water your sheep, and get the laugh
on me?

CORYDON

You can't know; that's the difficult thing about
it. Of course, you can't be sure; you have to
take my word for it—and I know just how you
feel. But one of us has to take a risk, or else,
why, don't you see? the game goes on forever.
It's terrible, when you stop to think of it. . . .
Oh, Thyrsis, now for the first time I feel this
wall is actually a wall—a thing come up between us—shutting me away from you. . . .
I do not know you any more!

THYRSIS

No, don't say that! Oh, Corydon, I'm willing
to drop it all, if you will! Come on over and
water your sheep! It is an ugly game. I hate
it from the first. . . . How did it start?

CORYDON

I do not know . . . I do not know. . . .
I think I am afraid of you! You are a stranger!
I never set eyes on you before! "Come over
and water my sheep," indeed! They'll be more
thirsty than they are now, before I bring them

over into your land, and have you mixing them up with yours, and calling them yours, and trying to keep them! *(Enter Columbine.)*

COLUMBINE

(to Cothurnus) Glummy, I want my hat.

THYRSIS

Take it, and go.

COLUMBINE

Take it and go, indeed! Is it my hat, or isn't it? Is this my scene, or not? Take it, and go! Really, you know you two are awfully funny! *(Exit Columbine.)*

THYRSIS

Corydon, my friend, I'm going to leave you now and whittle me a pipe, or sing a song, or go to sleep. When you have come to your senses, let me know. *(Goes back to where he has been sitting, lies down and sleeps.)* *(Corydon, in going back to where he has been sitting, stumbles over bowl of colored confetti and colored paper ribbons.)*

CORYDON

Why, what is this? Red stones—and purple stones—and stones stuck full of gold! The ground is full of gold and colored stones! . . . I'm glad the wall was up before I found them, otherwise I should have had to share them. As it is, they all belong to me. . . . Unless—*(He goes to wall and digs up and down the length of it, to see if there are jewels on the other side)* None here—none here—none here. They all belong to me! *(Sits.)*

THYRSIS *(awakening)*
How curious! I thought the little black lamb
came up and licked my hair! I saw the wool
about its neck as plain as anything! It must
have been a dream. The little black lamb is
on the other side of the wall, I'm sure. *(Goes
to wall and looks over. Corydon is seated on
the ground, tossing the confetti up into the air
and catching it)* Hello, what's that you've got
there, Corydon?

CORYDON
Jewels.

THYRSIS
Jewels? And where did you ever get them.

CORYDON
Oh, over here.

THYRSIS
You mean to say you found them by digging
around in the ground for them?

CORYDON *(unpleasantly)* No, Thyrsis; by digging down for water for my sheep.

THYRSIS
Corydon, come to the wall a minute, will you?
I want to talk to you.

CORYDON
I haven't time. I'm making me a necklace of
red stones.

THYRSIS
I'll give you all the water that you want for one
of those red stones—if it's a good one.

CORYDON
Water—what for—what do I want of water?

THYRSIS
Why, for your sheep!

CORYDON
My sheep? I'm not a shepherd!

THYRSIS
Your sheep are dying of thirst.

CORYDON
Man, haven't I told you I can't be bothered
with a few untidy brown sheep, all full of burdocks? I'm a merchant, that's what I am! And
I set my mind to it, I dare say I could be an
emperor! *(To himself)* Wouldn't I be a fool
to spend my time watching a flock of sheep go
up a hill, when I have these to play with—when
I have these to think about? I can't make up
my mind whether to buy a city, and have a thousand beautiful girls to bathe me, and be happy
until I die, or build a bridge, and name it the
Bridge of Corydon, and be remembered after
I'm dead.

THYRSIS
Corydon, come to the wall, won't you? I want
to tell you something.

CORYDON
Hush! Be off! Be off! Go finish your nap, I
tell you!

THYRSIS
Corydon, listen: if you don't want your sheep,
give them to me.

CORYDON
Be off! Go finish your nap! A red one—and a
blue one—and a red one—and a purple one.
Give you my sheep, did you say? Come, come!

What do you take me for, a fool? I've a lot
of thinking to do—and while I'm thinking the
sheep might just as well be over here as over
there. . . . A blue one—and a red one—

THYRSIS

But they will die!

CORYDON

And a green one—and a couple of white ones,
for a change.

THYRSIS

Maybe I have some jewels on my side.

CORYDON

And another green one—maybe, but I don't
think so. You see, this rock isn't so very wide.
It stops before it gets to the wall. It seems to
go quite deep, however.

THYRSIS *(with hatred)* I see.

COLUMBINE

(off stage) Look, Pierrot, there's the moon!

PIERROT

(off stage) Nonsense!

THYRSIS

I see.

COLUMBINE

(off stage) Sing me an old song, Pierrot—
something I can remember.

PIERROT

(off stage) Columbine, your mind is made of
crumbs—like an escallop of oysters—first a
layer of crumbs, and then an oyster taste, and
then a layer of crumbs.

THYRSIS

I find no jewels . . . but I wonder what the

63

root of this black weed would do to a man if
he should taste it. . . . I have seen a sheep
die, with half the stalk still drooling from its
mouth. 'Twould be a speedy remedy, I should
think, for a festered pride and a feverish ambi-
tion. It has a curious root. I think I'll hack it
in little pieces. . . . First I'll get me a drink;
and then I'll hack that root in little pieces as
small as dust, and see what the color is inside.
(Goes to bowl on floor) The pool is very clear.
I see a shepherd standing on the brink, with a
red cloak about him, and a black weed in his
hand. . . . 'Tis I. *(Kneels and drinks.)*

CORYDON

(coming to wall) Hello, what are you doing,
Thyrsis?

THYRSIS

Digging for gold.

CORYDON

I'll give you all the gold you want, if you'll give
me a bowl of water. If you don't want too
much, that is to say.

THYRSIS

Ho, so you've changed your mind! It's different, isn't it, when you want a drink yourself?

CORYDON

Of course it is.

THYRSIS

Well, let me see . . . a bowl of water—
come back in an hour, Corydon. I'm busy now.

CORYDON

Oh, Thyrsis, give me a bowl of water, and I'll
fill the bowl with jewels and bring it back!

THYRSIS

Be off, I'm busy now. *(He catches sight of the weed, picks it up and looks at it, unseen by Corydon)* Wait! Pick me out the finest stones you have. . . . I'll bring you a drink of water presently.

CORYDON

(goes back and sits down, with the jewels before him) A bowl of jewels is a lot of jewels.

THYRSIS

(chopping up the weed) I wonder if it has a bitter taste.

CORYDON

There's sure to be a stone or two among them I have grown fond of, pouring them from one hand into the other.

THYRSIS

I hope it doesn't taste too bitter, just at first.

CORYDON

A bowl of jewels is far too many jewels to give away . . . and not get back again.

THYRSIS

I don't believe he'll notice—he's thirsty—he'll gulp it down and never notice.

CORYDON

There ought to be some way to get them back again. . . . I could give him a necklace and snatch it back, after I'd drunk the water, I suppose . . . why, as for that, of course, a *necklace. . . . (He puts two or three of the colored tapes together and tries their strength by pulling them, after which he puts them around his neck and pulls them, gently, nodding*

5

*to himself. He gets up and goes to the wall,
with the colored tapes in his hands. Thyrsis in
the meantime has poured the powdered root—
black confetti—into the pot which contains the
flower and filled it up with wine from the punch-
bowl on the floor. He comes to the wall at the
same time, holding the bowl of poison.)*

THYRSIS

Come and get your bowl of water, Corydon.

CORYDON

Ah, very good! And for such a gift as that
I'll give you more than a bowl of unset stones.
I'll give you three long necklaces, my friend.
Come closer. Here they are. *(Puts the rib-
bons about Thyrsis' neck.)*

THYRSIS

(putting bowl to Corydon's mouth) I'll hold
the bowl until you've drunk it all.

CORYDON

Then hold it steady. For every drop you spill
I'll have a stone back out of this chain.

THYRSIS

I shall not spill a drop. *(Corydon drinks, mean-
while beginning to strangle Thyrsis)*

THYRSIS

Don't pull the string so tight.

CORYDON

You're spilling the water.

THYRSIS

You've had enough—you've had enough—stop
pulling the string so tight!

CORYDON

Why, that's not tight at all. . . . How's this?

66

THYRSIS

(drops bowl) You're strangling me! Oh, Corydon! It's only a game—and you are strangling me!

CORYDON

It's only a game, is it? Yet I believe you've poisoned me in earnest! *(Writhes and pulls the strings tighter, winding them about Thyrsis' neck.)*

THYRSIS

Corydon! *(Dies.)*

CORYDON

You've poisoned me in earnest. . . . I feel so cold. . . . So cold. . . . This is a very silly game. . . . Why do we play it? Let's not play this game a minute more. . . . Let's make a little song about a lamb. . . . I'm coming over the wall, no matter what you say —I want to be near you. . . . *(Groping his way, with arms wide before him, he strides through the frail papers of the wall without knowing it, and continues seeking for the wall straight across the stage)* Where is the wall? *(Gropes his way back, and stands very near Thyrsis without knowing it; he speaks slowly)* There isn't any wall, I think. *(Takes a step forward, his foot touches Thyrsis' body, and he falls down beside him)* Thyrsis, where is your cloak? Just give me a little bit of your cloak! *(Draws corner of Thyrsis' cloak over his shoulders, falls across Thyrsis' body and dies. Cothurnus closes the prompt-book with a bang, arises matter-of-factly, comes down stage,*

and places the table over the two bodies, draw-
ing down the cover so that they are hidden from
any actors on the stage, but visible to the audi-
ence, pushing in their feet and hands with his
boot. He then turns his back to the audience,
and claps his hands twice.)

COTHURNUS
Strike the scene! *(Exit Cothurnus. Enter*
Pierrot and Columbine.)

PIERROT
Don't puff so, Columbine!

COLUMBINE
Lord, what a mess this set is in! If there's one
thing I hate above everything else—even more
than getting my feet wet—it's clutter! He
might at least have left the scene the way he
found it . . don't you say so, Pierrot? *(She*
picks up punch bowl. They arrange chairs as
before at ends of table.)

PIERROT
Well, I don't know. I think it rather diverting
the way it is. *(Yawns, picks up confetti bowl)*
Shall we begin?

COLUMBINE *(screams)*
My God! What's that there under the table?

PIERROT
It is the bodies of the two shepherds from the
other play.

COLUMBINE *(slowly)*
How curious to strangle him like that with colored paper ribbons.

PIERROT
Yes, and yet I dare say he is just as dead.

68

(Pause. Calls Cothurnus) Come, drag these
bodies out of here! We can't sit down and eat
with two dead bodies lying under the table!
. . . The audience wouldn't stand for it!

COTHURNUS

(off stage) What makes you think so? Pull
down the tablecloth on the other play, and hide
them from the house, and play the farce. The
audience will forget.

PIERROT

That's so. Give me a hand there, Columbine.
*(Pierrot and Columbine pull down the table
cover in such a way that the two bodies are
hidden from the house, then merrily set their
bowls back on the table, draw up their chairs,
and begin the play exactly as before, speaking
even more rapidly and artificially.)*

COLUMBINE

Pierrot, a macaroon! I cannot *live* without a
macaroon!

PIERROT

My only love, you are *so* intense! . . . Is it
Tuesday, Columbine? I'll kiss you if it's Tuesday. *(Curtains begin to close slowly.)*

COLUMBINE

It is Wednesday, if you must know. . . . Is
this my artichoke, or yours?

PIERROT

Ah, Columbine, as if it mattered! Wednesday.
. . . Will it be Tuesday, then, to-morrow,
by any chance? . . .

[CURTAIN]

69

ㅎ토
　ㅊㅇㄴ

COCAINE

A PLAY IN ONE ACT

By Pendleton King

Copyright, 1920,
By Frank Shay

All Rights Reserved

Reprinted from No. 5 of "The Provincetown Plays" published by Frank Shay, by special permission of the publisher.

The professional and amateur stage rights on this play are strictly reserved by The Provincetown Players. Applications for permission to produce the play should be made to The Provincetown Players, 133 Macdougal St., New York.

Cocaine was first produced by The Provincetown Players, under the direction of Margaret Wycherly, on the night of March 9, 1917, with the following caste:

Joe	Eugene Lincoln
Nora	Ida Rauh

Scene designed and executed by Ira Remsen and Carroll Berry.

PERSONS

JOE
NORA

COCAINE

*The action takes place in an attic bed room on
Grand Street, between Allen and the Bowery,
in the late summer of 1916, and occupies the
time between four o'clock a. m. and daylight.
The ceiling slopes down at the back to within
a few feet of the floor. There is a dormer
window in a recess at back. Door left center,
bed at right of window, table left, bureau down
left, trunk down right, chair at foot of bed.
The room is in terrible disorder and confusion,
faintly seen in the glare from open window as
curtain rises.*

*Joe is discovered lying on the bed asleep, snoring
gently, dressed in undershirt and trousers. He
is good looking, powerfully built, twenty-four
years old.*

*Nora comes in and lights a candle on the bureau.
She is a wistful-looking girl of thirty.*

JOE

Nora, 's 'at you?

NORA

I didn't mean to wake you up. Go on back to
sleep.

JOE

I haven't been asleep. What time is it?

NORA

(takes off hat) About four o'clock.

73

JOE

You're pretty late.

NORA

(takes off jacket) Had to walk from uptown.

JOE

How far uptown?

NORA

O, way up town. I let a crowd shake me like a fool. *(Sits in chair at foot of bed and fans herself)* And didn't have sense enough to get car fare. Whew! You don't realize how hot you are till you sit down.

JOE

Poor kid.

NORA

You must have had the gas lighted to make it as hot as this in here. Lord, I'm so glad to get home.

JOE *(gently)*

You didn't bring in—nothing?

NORA

Not a cent, Joe. *(Gets up and goes to bureau)* I don't know what's the matter with me. *(Looks in glass)* It's that darn fever blister. If I had only had sense enough to get some camphor that first day.

JOE

But it's most well now. Can't hardly notice it any more.

NORA

Of course it's perfectly well. There won't be a trace of it to-morrow. I oughtn't to have tried to go out those two days the first of the week when it was so bad. Everybody was afraid of me and it made me feel like a leper. I lost my grip in some way and now I can't get it back. It all depends on yourself. *(Picks up candle)* If you're sure of yourself you have luck; if you aren't, you don't. That's all there is to it. *(Crosses with candle, which she puts down on trunk)* If I'd had a wee bit of a sniff to-night I'd have got some money out of that crowd. *(Sits on foot of the bed)* But drinks don't brace me up somehow.

JOE

Hum. 'sright.

NORA

Poor old boy. Have you been lying here all night in this heat waiting for me? It's hard luck on you, Joe. Oh, I thought I'd go crazy to-night! My nerves are just all to pieces. I did think I was going to get some money this time.

JOE

Why don't you take your clothes off and come on to bed?

NORA

(gets up and takes a packet of cigarettes out of her jacket) I swiped these for you, anyway. Here. *(Throws him the box.)*

JOE

(catching it) Gee! Ta!

NORA

Joe, I wish you wouldn't say "Ta." *(Goes up into recess)* I don't know why I hate it so. *(She begins to undress.)*

75

JOE

All right, Missis. *(Gets up to light his cigarette with the candle)* Common stuff, uhm?

NORA

(undressing) No, it doesn't matter. I'm just nervous and irritable. Don't pay any attention to anything I say. If I don't get some money to-morrow I just don't know what I'll do. It's terrible to be so dependent on *anything* as that.

JOE

(lies down again) Four days.

NORA

No, to-night's Saturday.

JOE

Well, that's four days, ain't it? We finished up that last deck Tuesday night.

NORA

That's right. I wouldn't have believed I could go so long. I don't see how you stand it, Joe, all night like this, doing nothing.

JOE

I been out. Don't worry about me. I can git on without de stuff—for awhile.

NORA

(comes down in kimono) I *can't.* *(Takes cigarette)* But then I've been using it so much longer than you have. *(Lights cigarette at the candle.)*

JOE

I been goin' it some little time—a month or so before we took up together last summer.

NORA

To think. *(Sits on bed)* Only a year. I wonder what would have become of you if I hadn't found you?

NORA

JOE

What becomes of all de other poor bastards who gets knocked out and can't get back in de ring? I don't know.

NORA

That's the trouble with you boys. You are brought up with only one idea—to fight—and if anything does happen to you, you're not fit to do anything else. You're only twenty-four, and you're done.

JOE

Be twenty-four in October, I guess.

NORA

Lord, it makes me feel so old. That's how you stand the strain the way you do. You are as firm and strong as you ever were, and look at me!

JOE

Well, if a fellow has to do as much trainin' as I used to, he more or less keeps in condition, I guess.

NORA

(lies down beside him) I feel so old, and tired, and discouraged, Joe. If I didn't have you I don't think I'd go on with it.

JOE

(tightens his arm about her) I'm stickin' to you, see?

NORA

I never thought of your leaving me. *(She puts her arm up about his head and strokes his hair)*

I love you too much, Joe. I love you more than anybody else will ever love you if you live to be a thousand years old.

JOE

I don't reckon anybody'd love me much if I was that old.

NORA *(laughs)*

I should. But you're only a baby now. A little old infant. *(She snuggles up to him and presses her cheek to his)* Joe?

JOE

Um?

NORA

(in a whisper) My darling. *(He gathers her closer. Long pause.)*

JOE

Tired, kid?

NORA

No, not now. I get strength from you. You've got plenty of strength for both of us, haven't you? Um?

JOE

It's funny, ain't it, for a girl like you to take up wid a rough guy like me, dat ain't never know'd nothin' but how to get his heart put on the blink! Dope brings funny people together.

NORA

Not so funny.

JOE

You needn't tell me, kid. I may be nothing but a prizefighter, but I can tell a lady when I see one. And, besides, you won't even own up to it. That's a sure sign.

NORA *(laughs)*

Not a very fine kind of a lady. I've told you all about myself. I did work on the *Evening Sun,* and before that I used to live on a farm in Kentucky. That's all there is.

JOE

Well, that's what you say. I don't want you to tell me nothing you don't want to. *(Moves his position slightly)* Are you all right?

NORA

Yes.

JOE

I got something I want to talk to you about. We're up against it.

NORA

I know we are. And yet I can lie here like this and it doesn't seem possible that there is such a thing as trouble in the world. It is so serene to lie still, and just stroke your hair. I don't want ever to move again. I can feel your heart beating. Do you feel how much faster mine is going than yours?

JOE

Yeah. *(The sound of the Elevated is heard.)*

NORA

The Elevated sounds like wind. Like a spirit that can't rest. The spirit of the city, that goes on and on day and night and never stops and never will stop, no matter what becomes of you and me. But when I am lying close to you like this, touching you, there's a sort of electric current that radiates from you all over because

79

you're so alive. What was I going to say?
What was I talking about?

JOE
You was talking about the El.

NORA
Yes. I was going to say while I am lying close
to you like this it all seems so far away, doesn't
it? It is like lying snug in bed and listening to
the sea. There may be death and storms and
shipwrecks and things out there, but they're far
away. They can never touch us.

JOE
I wisht we could get a good old sniff, and forget our troubles right.

NORA
Poor old Joe. *(Raises up and sits on the side
of the bed again)* I declare I thought I would
go crazy to-night; I haven't got a nerve left in
my body. I wanted to know what you were
doing. I thought all sorts of fool things. I
could picture you getting desperate and breaking in somewhere and getting locked up, and
I don't know what.

JOE
I could have got some stuff to-night, at that.

NORA
What do you mean? How? Who?

JOE
The landlady. She was up here talking to me
about it.

NORA
When she knows how broke we are? We owe
her two weeks' rent.

JOE

No, I guess she would have give me some.

NORA

How do you mean, Joe?

JOE

You know.

NORA

Do you mean to tell me that woman has been up here after you again? *(Her eyes narrow)* I knew something was the matter. Did you— What did you tell her?

JOE

Told her to get to hell out of here. What do you think I told her? I said I was off de stuff.

NORA

(buries her head in his shoulder) O, Joe.

JOE

Well, I didn't want it so bad, then. She come up here when she heard me come in, about twelve o'clock, and put it up to me.

NORA *(desperate)*

If we had any other place on earth we could go, I would have got out of this house the night you told me she first came up here and bothered you. But we couldn't get another place. She'd hold our things until we paid her. And I haven't got a dollar to deposit on a room. I suppose she knows all that.

JOE

That's what I got to talk to you about. She's going to kick us out.

NORA

Kick us out?

JOE

That's what she says.   Unless—

NORA

Unless what?

JOE

Well—you know—I been thinking pretty hard
and figurin' on puttin' it up to you, if you think
it's worth while—just to keep the room on and
have a place to sleep.   You see—

NORA

What are you talking about?

JOE

Well, I think the old lady's reasonable.   She
come up here and made a big fuss over me and
said she was gone on me and all that stuff, and
I was staying on in her house and not paying
no rent and everything, and—if I was too good
for her I'd have to get out of her house, that's
all.   That was after she offered me the dope.

NORA

Joe, am I mad or what are you talking about?

JOE

Well—

NORA

Never let me hear that again.   Do you think
I'd let you—

JOE

Well, I let you, don't I?

NORA

That's altogether a different matter.   Don't
ever let me hear that again, do you understand?
I can't argue about it.   (*Gets up and crosses
to bureau*)   God, it's hot in here!

JOE

(swings his feet out and sits on the side of the bed. Kindly) Now look here, kid. *(Stands a moment and goes over to her)* I got to live, ain't I? You are the swellest little girl any fellow ever had and all that, and I'm awful fond of you, but we got to live. We got to do something. We got to get some money some way. If we can't get on—the way we been gettin' on—then I got to shift for myself, see? *(Takes her by the shoulders)* I'm putting it up to you square, because I'm goin' to be straight with you.

NORA

Of course we've got to do something. I'll do something. I'll get some money. You don't understand what you are saying. If it were the last night we'd ever spend under a roof it wouldn't alter the question.

JOE

(turns back to the bed) By God, it looks like it is the last night, with the luck you're having. *(He sits and leans his chin on his right hand, gazing at the candle)* If I was able to do any kind of work it'd be different. But de stuff's got me, I guess. I couldn't no more stick to any kind of a job than I could fly. You reckon if I was able to get back in the ring I'd have you working? But we're up against it, that's all. As long as you can bring in the money— all right. But you ain't having any luck, and I just got to do it, that's all. If I'm willing for you to go out every night, I don't

83

see why you kick on one old measly land-lady.

NORA

But, Joe, you don't understand. *(Crosses to bed)* Listen to me. *(Sits beside him)* You don't love me the way I do you. It isn't your fault. It's the way you're made. I can—go out, as you call it—It's a sort of sacrifice to you, a sort of way of showing how much I love you. It doesn't matter about me. You are the clean part of me. You are part I live for. And you are sacred, do you understand? Clean.

JOE

(Still gazing at candle) Sure, I get you. *(Nora slips down on one knee and buries her face against his arm)* And I've always been straight with you. I think a whole lot more of you than you think.

NORA

Go on. Say you love me. I love to hear you say it.

JOE

(puts his left arm about her) I love you all right. And I'll stick to you. But we got to live, ain't we? We got to get some money some way. And if you can't get it, I got to. That's if we're going to stick together.

NORA

No, you haven't, Joe. I'd rather be dead. *(Raises up)* I'll starve to death before I'll see you do that, and let you starve to death. *(Gets up)* The horrible old slut. I think I'll kill her. *(Goes up into alcove and looks out of window.)*

JOE

O, we can get out of here if you want to. It don't have to be her. There's more'n one way of pickin' up money round this town.

NORA

(turns toward him) What do you mean?

JOE

I guess you must know. It's the only way I see. I ain't got nothing but my looks.

NORA

(turns back to window) Joe, don't talk like that, *please.*

JOE *(kindly)*

We got to, kid. We're up against it. I'm going to be fair with you; that thing you got on your mouth ain't going to get well so as you can't see it for two or three days yet. We get kicked out of here to-day. What the hell can we do? Sleep in the park? I guess not. Not while I got a way to make easy money. Why, kid, I wisht you'd see the number of 'em tries to speak to me every time I go out. It's easy, I tell you. And there's good money in it. I don't like to talk about it——'specially with you ——but we got to——if we're going to stick to-gether. We can get a nice room somewheres and keep a little stuff on hand all the time. I ain't going to leave you. But I gotta have de stuff, that's all. *(Lies down on the bed and turns toward the wall)* I've gone without it four days now.

85

NORA

(comes down and crosses to trunk) You are a strange boy. *(Sits on end of trunk facing him)* Can't you see that you are the only thing I've got left in the world?

JOE

But I ain't leaving you, I tell you.

NORA

Don't you understand that I found you when you were down and out—done for? That you belong to me? I saved you from this very thing, I suppose, a year ago. Don't you see, darling?

JOE

(turns on his back) But I'm not— Gee, Nora, can't you listen to me? I don't want to do it, kid, but we got to, to live.

NORA

But don't you understand that I wouldn't touch you with a ten-foot pole afterwards? Don't you see that?

JOE

(turning back in a huff) Of course, if you feel that way about it, we can bust up, 's far as that goes. If you don't think no more about me than that.

NORA

(stands up against the wall. Right) Don't, Joe.

JOE

(sits up in bed) I've always been straight with you. I've treated you right all the way, and I'm trying to stick by you. But of course, if

86

that's the way you feel about it, all right.   I
got to live, ain't I?

NORA

No.

JOE

What do you mean by no?

NORA

I don't see any reason why we should live.

JOE

Well, I'm *going* to live.

NORA

*(sits down on bed and tries to turn him towards
her)* Joe, my darling, listen to me.   You've
been a wonderful boy, and I love you as very
few people have ever been loved in this world.
Because I had lost everything, you see, when
I found you, everything.   I had thrown everything away.   And you've had to be the whole
world for me since.   The whole world, you see.
There isn't anything else.   When the dope got
me I just went down because I didn't care about
anything.   I gave up my job and just let myself
slide.   I intended to kill myself when my money
gave out, and I didn't even care how much I
had left.   Then I found you that night at
Mitchell's place.

JOE

(turns on his back) I remember.

NORA

(Puts her head down on his chest) You can't
remember much.   I can't bear to think even
now how you were beat up.   But you were so
full of it you didn't know your arm was broken.

JOE

That's right. I think it was broke about two days before that. I remember when it went.

NORA

And since then, Joe, we've had a wonderful time. Do you remember when we used to have to sleep under the Bridge? I love that old Bridge now because it's associated in my mind with you.

JOE

We had a good time, all right.

NORA *(straightens up)*

"But now the white sails of our ship are furled,
  And spent the lading of our argosy."

We've come to the end of our tether, Joe.

JOE

Um.

NORA

What do you say we don't go on with it?

JOE

What do you mean don't go on with it?

NORA

Turn on the gas.

JOE

(sits up) Nix! What are you gettin' at? *(Lies down)* Not for mine.

NORA

Joe, we've had such a wonderful time. We've known everything there is to know in the world worth knowing. Don't let's go down hill. We've reached the top. Let's let this be the end. I can't keep you any longer and have got to let you go. And I won't do it, that's all.

88

JOE

(sits up and props himself against the head of the bed incredulously) You must be kiddin'. Aw, come on.

NORA *(quietly)*

I never was more serious in my life. I can't go on with it, and I won't leave you behind to live without me. It's you that I love—the little strange spirit that makes you you, and different to everybody else that ever lived. If you go on you are going to destroy that. Then you won't be you, and I won't love you any more. Think! This may be the last night we'll ever spend together—the last chance we'll have. Let's turn it on now. No telling *(she turns front)* what'll happen in the daylight to-morrow. I can't wait to face it.

JOE

I don't want to, kid. It ain't right to kill yourself.

NORA

Are you afraid to die?

JOE

Sure I'm not afraid to die.

NORA

What have you got to live for?

JOE

Well, a lot of things, I guess.

NORA

Joe, you've slipped. You've slipped away further than I thought. The stuff's got you sure enough. You've slipped further than I have.

89

JOE

I guess not. I'm not so bad off as that.

NORA *(slightly hysterical)*

You're pretty bad off, Joe. Don't you see that your life is finished. You are nothing. You are less than nothing. What you really are is the lowest thing that can be on earth, and here you talk calmly about—something even worse. There's no reason for you to go on living—except your fear of death.

JOE

I'm not afraid of dying, I tell you.

NORA *(rising)*

Well, let me turn on the gas, then. I'm not afraid. Look at me. Think of the trouble it takes to live. Think of the effort to keep yourself going on and on, like a rat in a trap. And when you lose me you'll just slip and slip. And you've got to die in the end anyhow. And when you're dead it won't make any difference to you how long you lived. It will be just as if you'd never been born.

JOE

(sits up and follows her with his eyes) I don't get you.

NORA

O, I just can't face the daylight again, Joe. I'm too tired. Aren't you tired? What will become of you without me to take care of you? *(She is edging towards the gas jet in the alcove.)*

JOE

I don't know.

NORA

Let's turn on the gas. Then we won't have to wake up in the morning and be bothered. And you can't tell—maybe— But I believe you're scared.

JOE

(lies down and turns face to the wall petulantly) Aw, turn on your God-damned gas. I'll show you whether I'm scared.

NORA

(in an excited whisper) O, Joe!
(She closes the window and hangs an old skirt over it, turns on the gas jet and the gas stove on the table, then comes down on tiptoe, trembling, and blows out the candle on the trunk. The stage is completely dark.)

JOE

Did you turn it on?

NORA

(gets back into the bed) Yes; the stove, too.

JOE

How long will it take?

NORA

Not long, I think. I don't know. Don't let's talk about it. Joe, do you think I've got the right to take you with me?

JOE

With you? Where?

NORA

Now—like this. But I couldn't bear for anybody else to have you, Joe.

JOE
    Gee, you're tremblin'.   I believe you're scared
    now.
NORA
    I'm not scared.   I'm just happy.
JOE
    Happy?
NORA
    I thought I'd lost you, Joe.
JOE
    Um.   *(Very long pause)*   This is a tough thing
    to do, all right, kid.   You reckon they'll put it
    in the papers?
NORA
    I expect so.
JOE
    Will they put in much?   They'll be sure to find
    out who we was.   You got letters and stuff in
    the trunk.
NORA
    We weren't anybody much.   I expect they've
    forgotten about us.
JOE
    Aw, they got to put it in the papers.
NORA
    They'll put in something.   Please don't let's
    talk about it.   Joe?
JOE
    Um?
NORA
    (in a whisper)   My darling!
    (Long pause.)

92

JOE

(with a tremor in his voice) I don't smell no gas.

NORA

It hasn't had time yet. Maybe we won't smell it.

JOE

Gee, we got to smell it. *(The bed creaks)* I don't smell nothing way down here.

NORA

Just wait and you will. It's only been on a minute. O, Joe, come on back here. We've only got such a little while.

JOE

I'm going to see what's the matter. Gimme a match. *(The bed creaks as he gets out.)*

NORA

For heaven's sake, don't strike a match! Might be an explosion!

JOE

It can't blow up if you can't smell it. *(He finds matches on the trunk and crosses to center stage)* I can smell it over here. *(Strikes a match to the gas burner, which lights in a feeble blue flame)* Gee, the meter's run out on us!

NORA

(sits up in bed) The meter? But it can't have run out. *(A wave of terror comes over her)* Have you been using the gas nights?

JOE

Not but very little.

NORA

But that's ridiculous. I haven't got a quarter to put in it. What can we do?

JOE

Nothin'—'less we had a quarter.

NORA *(laughs)*

But that's ridiculous. We've got to do something.

JOE

Naw, I guess not.

NORA

But, Joe—!!!

JOE

(with a note of relief in his voice) Naw, I guess it wasn't meant for us to kick out to-night, kid. *(Gently)* Let's get the window open. *(He takes down the old skirt and opens the window. The dawn has come up outside)* Gee, it's daylight.

[CURTAIN]

NIGHT

A DRAMA

By James Oppenheim

Copyright, 1918,
By Egmont Arens

All Rights Reserved

NIGHT *was first produced by the Provincetown Players on November 2, 1917, with the following cast;*

THE SCIENTIST, *Justus Sheffield*
THE POET, *George Cram Cook*
THE PRIEST, *Hutchinson Collins*
THE MAN, *Rollo Peters*
THE WOMAN, *Ida Rauh*

The scene and method of playing, suggested by Rollo Peters. The actors appear in silhouette before a lighted blue screen upon a simple mound that suggests a hilltop.

NIGHT

A Priest, A Poet, A Scientist.
Hilltop, in October; the stars shining.

(The Priest kneels; the Scientist looks at the
heavens through a telescope; the Poet writes
in a little note-book.)

THE PRIEST

When I consider Thy heavens, the work of Thy
    fingers, the moon and the stars, which
    Thou hast ordained;
What is man, that Thou art mindful of him,
And the son of man, that Thou visitest him?

THE SCIENTIST

Algol which is dim, becomes again a star of
    the second magnitude.

THE POET

My beloved is far from this hilltop, where the
    firs breathe heavily, and the needles fall;
But from the middle of the sea
She, too, gazes on the lustrous stars of calm
    October, and in her heart
She stands with me beneath these heavens—
    daintily blows
Breath of the sighing pines, and from the
    loaded and bowed-down orchards and
    from the fields
With smokes of the valley, peace steps up on
    this hill.

7

THE PRIEST

    Thou art the Shepherd that strides down the
        Milky Way;

    Thou art the Lord, our God: glorified be Thy
        name and Thy works.

    I see Thee with Thy staff driving the star-
        sheep to the fold of dawn.

THE SCIENTIST

    The Spiral Nebula in Ursa Major, that forever
        turns

    Slowly like a flaming pin-wheel...thus are
        worlds born;

    Thus was the sun and all the planets a handful
        a million years ago.

THE POET

    She is far from me...but in the cradle of the
        sea

    Sleepless she rocks, calling her beloved: he
        heeds her call:

    On this hilltop he picks the North Star for his
        beacon...

    For by that star the sailors steer, and beneath
        that star

    She and I are one in the gaze of the heavens.

THE PRIEST

    (Slowly rising and turning to the others.)

    Let us glorify the Creator of this magnificence
        of infinite Night,

    His footstool is the Earth, and we are but the
        sheep of this Shepherd.

THE SCIENTIST

    Thus shall we only glorify ourselves,

That of this energy that rolls and drives in
    suns and planets
Are but the split-off forces with cunning brains,
And questioning consciousness. . . Pray if you
    must—
Only your own ears hear you, and only the
    heart in your breast
Responds to the grandiose emotion. . . See yon-
    der star?
That is the great Aldebaron, great in the night,
Needing a whole sky, as a vat and a reservoir,
    which he fills with his flame. . .
But no astronomer with his eye to his lenses
Has seen ears on the monster.

THE PRIEST
    Thou that hast never seen an atom, nor the
        ether thou pratest of,
    Thou that hast never seen the consciousness of
        man,
    What knowest thou of the invisible arms about
        this sky,
    And the Father that leans above us?

THE POET
    We need know nothing of any Father
    When the grasses themselves, withering in Oc-
        tober, stand up and sing their own dirges
        in the great west wind,
    And every pine is like a winter lodging house
        where the needles may remember the
        greenness of the world,
    And the great shadow is jagged at its top with
        stars,

And the heart of man is as a wanderer looking
    for the light in a window,
And the kiss and warm joy of his beloved.

THE PRIEST

    Man of Song and Man of Science,
    Truly you are as people on the outside of a
        house,
    And one of you only sees that it is made of
        stone, and its windows of glass, and that
        fire burns in the hearth,
    And the other of you sees that the house is
        beautiful and very human,
    But I have gone inside the house,
    And I live with the host in that house
    And have broken bread with him, and drunk
        his wine,
    And seen the transfiguration that love and awe
        make in the brain...
    For that house is the world, and the Lord is
        my host and my father:
    It is my father's house.

THE SCIENTIST

    He that has gone mad and insane may call him-
        self a king,
    And behold himself in a king's palace, with
        feasting, and dancing women, and with
        captains,
    And none can convince him that he is mad,
    Slave of hallucination...
    We that weigh the atom and weigh a world in
        the night, and we
    Who probe down into the brain, and see how
        desire discolors reality,

And we that see how chemical energy changes
   and transforms the molecule,
So that one thing and another changes and so
   man arises—
With neither microscope, nor telescope, nor
   spectroscope, nor finest violet ray
Have we found any Father lurking in the in-
   tricate unreasonable drive of things
And the strange chances of nature.

THE POET

O Priest, is it not enough that the world and
   a Woman are very beautiful,
And that the works and tragic lives of men are
   terribly glorious?
There is a dance of miracles, of miracles holding hands in a chain around the Earth and
   out through space to the moon, and to the
   stars, and beyond the stars,
And to behold this dance is enough;
So much laughter, and secret looking, and
   glimpses of wonder, and dreams of terror...
It is enough! It is enough!

THE PRIEST

Enough? I see what is enough!
Machinery is enough for a Scientist,
And Beauty is enough for a Poet;
But in the hearts of men and women, and in
   the thirsty hearts of little children
There is a hunger, and there is an unappeas-
   able longing,
For a Father and for the love of a Father...
For the root of a soul is mystery,

And the Night is mystery,
And in that mystery men would open inward
    into Eternity,
And know love, the Lord.
Blessed be his works, and his angels, and his
    sons crowned with his glory!
    *(A pause. The Woman with a burden in her
    arms comes in slowly.)*

THE WOMAN
Who has the secret of life among you?

THE PRIEST
I, woman, have that secret:
I have learned it from the book of the revela-
    tions of God,
And I have learned it from life, bitterly,
And from my heart, holily.

THE SCIENTIST
Be not deceived, woman:
There is only one book of reality—the book of
    Nature.

THE WOMAN
Who has read in that book?

THE SCIENTIST
I have read a little:
No man has read much.

THE POET
They lead you nowhere, woman;
You are the secret of life, and your glory is in
    seeking the secret,
But finding it never.

THE WOMAN
I have climbed this hill and found three
    watchers of the night—

Three star-gazers perched above the placid
   October harvests
Where they lie golden and crimson along the
   valley, and high on the slopes
The scarlet maples flame—
You are a priest: and you speak of God.
I am nothing but need: for I carry a burden
   that is heavier than the Earth, and is
   heavier
Than the flesh of woman can bear: I break
Down under it: and a hard hate
Against my birth is steel in my heart—I curse
God, if there be a God—
Love, if there ever was love—
Life, that is empty ravings,
And the hour when I was born.

THE PRIEST
   Peace! Peace! Thou standest in the presence
      of the Night
   Shadowy with grace and benediction—the
      mercy
   Of the Lord falls like the dew on the soft brow
      of thy affliction!

THE POET (*softly*)
   She is very beautiful and dark with her stern
      cursing,
   Standing there like an enemy of great Jehovah,
   A demon-woman satanic—she is very beautiful,
   With her arms full of her burden, and the stars
   Seeming to retreat before her.

THE SCIENTIST
   What burden is that you carry?

THE WOMAN

    That which is worth nothing,

    And worth more than these stars you gaze at.

THE PRIEST

    Put thy burden upon the Lord, and thy trust
        in His loving kindness.

THE WOMAN

    I will not part with my burden, though it is
        worth nothing...

    For what are a few pounds of dead flesh worth
        when the life has left it?

THE PRIEST

    Then you carry the dead at your breast?

THE WOMAN

    I carry the dead...

THE PRIEST

    Flesh of your flesh and bone of your bone...

THE WOMAN

    My breasts are still heavy with unsucked
        milk...

THE PRIEST

    Your child has died...

THE WOMAN

    My baby is dead...

THE PRIEST

    The Lord giveth, the Lord taketh away;

    Blessed be the name of the Lord.

THE WOMAN

    Nine long months

    I ripened with the human seed, and like a goodly
        tree that is green

    Stooped with sheltering boughs above the swell-
        ing fruit...

Song rang sweetly in my blood...
I tasted the silent life as a spring hillside
    where the furrows are run
So holds its bated breath against the pressing
    of the grass-blades
That birds coming that way catch the held-
    down glory under the furrows
And scatter ecstatic golden notes in the morn-
    ing light...
Until the trumpets blasted, as if the opening
    heavens of a sunrise
Were battalions of bright trumpeters blowing
    news of dawn...
Sank I then into darkness,
Sank I then into terror,
Till I was healed of pain by the new-born, my
    child...
And now, behold in my arms
The life of my life:
All that I was went out in him: my life was
    now outside me.

THE PRIEST
    Unto thee a son was born!

THE WOMAN
    I ran to tend him with glad feet, and with
       laughter...
    For my life was now outside of me,
    And I was seeking my life.

THE PRIEST
    You praised the Lord?

THE WOMAN
    I loved my child...

THE PRIEST
  And God forgotten?
THE WOMAN
   That child was holy...
THE PRIEST
  He was but flesh...
THE WOMAN
  Just so was Christ...
THE PRIEST
  A Son of God...
THE WOMAN
  My child was such...
THE PRIEST
  So in the corrupt new generations of men
  They forget God, and love but the flesh,
  And the corruptible flesh decays after its kind
  And in their bereavement they have nothing
      ...then in their sorrow
  They curse the true and the good.
THE WOMAN
  The flesh, you say?   Here is the flesh:
  But was it the flesh when his blue eyes opened
      and gazed with great hunger,
  Was it the flesh that wailed, the flesh that
      warmed against my naked breasts, the flesh
  That went a secret way, and I after, I after,
      seeking through embraces
  To catch my son back, hold him...but, oh,
      he was gone,
  He was gone, leaving *this*. Priest, is this all
      you have for the bereaved?
THE PRIEST
  That which is gone is now with God.

THE WOMAN

I was his God, for to me the beautiful bright
life raised its hands,
Suppliant, full of faith...
He wailed for enfolding love: I gave it
For daily bread: I gave it
For healing and shelter: I gave it.
Out of me he came, but away from me he has
gone,
And if he has found out some other mother,
I curse her in my jealousy!

THE PRIEST

So you blaspheme the holiness of the Omnipo-
tent!

THE WOMAN

So I curse the thief who stole my treasure away.

THE PRIEST

Alas! Who may speak to a sacrilegious gen-
eration?

THE WOMAN

Speak if you can, and tell me in a few words
What is the secret of life?

THE PRIEST

Life is a mysterious preparation for immor-
tality...
We are sons and daughters of God, who shall
later be angels, and in heaven
Know bliss beyond all dream.

THE WOMAN *(uncovering her child's face)*

My son...
You and I lately pulsed with one pulse, and
sang together one song:

For you the flaming pain, for you the terror
of birth...
And this priest's God let you suffer, in a glori-
ous preparation,
And let you die...(*Kisses him.*)
Cold! Cold! My heart tightens hard, my
blood is chilled...(*In a loud cry.*)
Hellish heaven! Devilish God!
(*Silence. The Poet advances and covers the
face.*)

THE POET
You are very wonderful and very noble in your
satanic anger,
Your curses are cleansing, for it is a mighty
thing for man to confront creation
Greater even than this vast Night, to stand in
his transiency
And his pitiful helplessness, and in the grasp
of his doom, and against death,
Darkness, and mysterious powers, alone of all
life
Godlike, downing the universe with defiance!
O godlike
Are you; and you *are* God!

THE WOMAN (*gazing at him*)
Who are you, with these words?

THE POET
Seer and singer, one who glories in life, and
through vision
Creates his own worlds.

THE WOMAN
Has your mother ever wept for you?

THE POET
  All mothers weep...
THE WOMAN
  Have you ever had a child?
THE POET
  No child of my own: but I know the love of
      children.
THE WOMAN
  Can I trust you with a great trust?
THE POET
  I think of you as a holy thing.
THE WOMAN
  Then—take this a moment,
  And feel how light a heavy burden may be.
  (She carefully places the child in his arms.)
THE POET
  How strangely light!
THE WOMAN
  You tremble. Why?
THE POET
  There is something so real in the stiff posture
      of these tiny legs,
  These crooked arms, this little body,
  This hanging head...
THE WOMAN
  Can you see him?
THE POET *(looking close)*
  O tiniest budding mouth,
  O dark deep fringes of eyelids,
  O pallid cheeks...
THE WOMAN
  And the little tuft of hair—you see it?

THE POET
> Take him! My heart is in despair!

THE WOMAN
> No one will have my burden; for my burden is heavier
> Than any save a mother can bear...O Earth, hard Earth,
> I shall not go mad: I hold back: I shut the doors on the Furies:
> I stand straight and stiff! I hold against my heart with words!
> *(Silence.)*
> So, poet, you are hushed! Life is too much for you!
> Go—live in your dreams and let the reality of experience
> Flow over you, untasted...You are wise: it is better!
> *(Silence.)*
> What? All silent? My star-gazers brought to a pause?
> You, too?

THE SCIENTIST *(grimly)*
> Who would listen to me must be hard and strong.

THE WOMAN
> Am I soft and weak?

THE SCIENTIST
> You have the strength of revolt, but not the greater strength of acceptance.

THE WOMAN
> What shall I accept?

THE SCIENTIST
  The inexorable facts of life.

THE WOMAN
  And what are those facts?

THE SCIENTIST
  That man is no more than the grasses, and that
    man is no more,
  Though his dreams are grandiose, than the
    pine on this hill, or the bright star
  Burning blue out yonder—strangely the chem-
    icals mix, and the forces interplay,
  And out of it consciousness rises, an energy
    harnessed by energies,
  And a little while it burns, then flickers, then
    vanishes out,
  And is no more than the October wind and the
    smell of dried hay.

THE WOMAN
  These are the facts?

THE SCIENTIST
  These are the facts.

THE WOMAN
  And my child was nothing but energy, gathered
    and scattered?

THE SCIENTIST
  These are the facts...

THE WOMAN
  He was only a cunning engine and a curious
    machine?

THE SCIENTIST
  Thus are we all...

THE WOMAN
  Not all...thus are *you*...

But this child was mine; he was my baby and
  he was my son.
And I was his life-giver, and his lover, and his
  mother...
And I knew the glory of this child, for I lived
  with it,
And I know the marvel and mystery of mother-
  hood, for I lived it...
I lived it, who now live the death of a treasured
  being,
And who know now that the light of the world
  is out, and only death
May heal me of anguish, and only death's long
  sleep
Shall bury my bereavement in peace...O
  mouthers of words,
Dreamers who do not live, I go back to the
  valley,
And there I shall put this babe in the Earth
  where the seeds of Autumn are sinking,
And there I shall slay myself, knowing that
  no one knows,
And no one helps, and life is a madness and a
  horror,
And to be dead is better than to suffer.

  *(They say nothing.   The Priest silently
    prays.   The Woman turns, and starts
    slowly out.   But as she goes a Man en-
    ters, searchingly.)*

THE MAN
  Beloved!   O where have you fled from me?

THE WOMAN
Go back—I hate you for bringing this being
    into life,
Whose loss has ruined life, life itself: and I
    had better never loved you,
For love brings children to the mother.

THE MAN
It is my child, too...I, too, have lost him.

THE WOMAN
You have lost a plaything and the promise of
    a man,
And you have lost a trouble and a burden:
But I have lost my love, and I have lost the life
    of my life.

THE MAN
You are cruel in your sorrow beyond all
    women...

THE WOMAN
Then leave me, and seek comfort elsewhere.
There are many women.

THE MAN
You are desperate, and there is a hardness in
    you that makes me afraid.
Where are you going?

THE WOMAN
I follow this child.

THE MAN
Then I lose *my* child...even as you lost yours.

THE WOMAN
Your child? Ha! I am gone!
    (Tries to pass him; he seizes her.)

8

THE MAN
> You shall not go, for you are mine.   O beloved,
> hear me!

THE WOMAN
> Take away your hands, for every moment that
> you make me stay
> Deepens my hate of you.

THE MAN
> You would break my life in bits?

THE WOMAN
> Your life is not so easily broken...
> You are a man...Come! I shall do some ter-
> rible thing—

THE MAN
> Then I, too, shall follow...

THE WOMAN
> Follow? Where?

THE MAN
> Wherever you go.

THE WOMAN
> Down into death?

THE MAN
> Even into death.
> *(A pause; she draws back a little.)*

THE WOMAN
> Are you crying?   Are there tears on your
> cheeks?
> Why do you heave so?

THE MAN
> Your love has died...

THE WOMAN
> Are you so weak?

THE MAN
  But I need you so...
THE WOMAN *(in a changed voice)*
  You need me!
THE MAN
  Look! I do not need you, who am alone, un-
    comforted,
  With no place on Earth, no life, no light, if
    you are gone...
THE WOMAN
  You need me?
THE MAN
  I need you...
    (Silence.)
THE WOMAN
  This man is my child...
    (Silence.)
THE MAN
    (Drawing her tenderly close.)
  Our dead child between us,
  O my beloved, is there not a future?
  May no more children issue from us, no more
    children
  Lovely, golden, waking with laughter, and
    clothed as with dawn
  With the memory of the dead? Come, my
    beloved,
  Down to the Valley, down to the living, down
    to the toilers.
  Come, my beloved! I am your child and your
    father,
  Your husband and your lover! Come, let us
    go!

THE WOMAN *(weeping)*
O my heart!
Something has broken in me, and the flood
flows through my being!
I come! I come!
*(They go out together, the Man with his arm
around the Woman.)*

THE PRIEST
Forgive these children, Lord God!

THE SCIENTIST
Ignorance is indeed bliss!

THE POET
The secret of life?
He gives it to her, she gives it to him...
But who shall tell of it? Who shall know it?

[CURTAIN]

ENEMIES

A PLAY

By Neith Boyce and Hutchins Hapgood

ENEMIES

As Produced by the Provincetown Players, New York City

HE, *Justus Sheffield*
SHE, *Ida Rauh*

SCENE—*A Living-room*
TIME—*After Dinner*

Produced by the Authors

Setting designed by B. J. O. Nordfeldt

ENEMIES

She is lying in a long chair, smoking a cigarette and reading a book. He is sitting at a table with a lamp at his left—manuscript pages scattered before him, pen in hand. He glances at her, turns the lamp up, turns it down, rustles his MS., snorts impatiently. She continues reading.

HE
  This is the limit!
SHE *(calmly)*
  What is?

HE
  Oh, nothing. *(She turns the page, continues reading with interest)* This is an infernal lamp!

SHE
  What's the matter with the lamp?

HE
  I've asked you a thousand times to have some order in the house, some regularity, some system! The lamps never have oil, the wicks are never cut, the chimneys are always smoked! And yet you wonder that I don't work more! How can a man work without light?

SHE
  (glancing critically at lamp) This lamp seems to me to be all right. It obviously has oil in it or it would not burn, and the chimney is not

smoked. As to the wick, I trimmed it myself to-day.

HE

Ah, that accounts for it!

SHE

Well, do it yourself next time, my dear!

HE *(irritated)*

But our time is too valuable for these ever-recurring jobs! Why don't you train Theresa, as I've asked you so often?

SHE

It would take all my time for a thousand years to train Theresa.

HE

Oh, I know! All you want to do is to lie in bed for breakfast, smoke cigarettes, write your high literary stuff, make love to other men, talk cleverly when you go out to dinner and never say a word to me at home! No wonder you have no time to train Theresa!

SHE

Is there anything of interest in the paper?

HE

You certainly have a nasty way of making an innocent remark!

HE

I'm sorry. *(Absorbed in her book.)*

HE

No, you're not. The last remark proves it.

SHE *(absently)*

Proves what?

HE

Proves that you are an unsocial, brutal woman!

SHE

You are in a temper again.

HE

Who wouldn't be, to live with a cold-blooded person that you have to hit with a gridiron to get a rise out of?

SHE

I wish you would read your paper quietly and let me alone.

HE

Why have you lived with me for fifteen years if you want to be let alone?

SHE *(with a sigh)*

I have always hoped you would settle down.

HE

By settling down you mean cease bothering about household matters, about the children, cease wanting to be with *you,* cease expecting you to have any interest in *me.*

SHE

No, I only mean it would be nice to have a peaceful evening sometimes. But *(laying book down)* I see you want to quarrel—so what shall we quarrel about? Choose your own subject, my dear.

HE

When you're with Hank you don't want a peaceful evening!

SHE

Now how can you possibly know that?

HE

Oh, I've seen you with him and others and I know the difference. When you're with them

121

you're alert and interested. You keep your unsociability for me. *(Pause)* Of course, I know why.

SHE

One reason is that "they" don't talk about lampwicks and so forth. They talk about higher things.

HE

Some people would call them lower things!

SHE

Well—more interesting things, anyway.

HE

Yes, I know you think those things more interesting than household and children and husband.

SHE

Oh, only occasionally, you know—just for a change. You like a change yourself sometimes.

HE

Yes, sometimes. But I am excited, and interested and keen whenever I am with you. It is not only cigarettes and flirtation that excite me.

SHE

Well, you are an excitable person. You get excited about nothing at all.

HE

Are home and wife and children nothing at all?

SHE

There are other things. But you, Deacon, are like the skylark—

"Type of the wise who soar but do not roam—
   True to the kindred points of heaven and
      home."

HE

You are cheaply cynical! You ought not to insult Wordsworth. He meant what he said.

SHE

He was a good man. . . . But to get back to our original quarrel. You're quite mistaken. I'm more social with you than with anyone else. Hank, for instance, hates to talk—even more than I do. He and I spend hours together looking at the sea—each of us absorbed in our own thoughts—without saying a word. What could be more peaceful than that?

HE *(indignantly)*

I don't believe it's peaceful—but it must be wonderful!

SHE

It is—marvelous. I wish you were more like that. What beautiful evenings we could have together!

HE *(bitterly)*

Most of our evenings are silent enough—unless we are quarreling!

SHE

Yes, if you're not talking, it's because you're sulking. You are never sweetly silent—never really quiet.

HE

That's true—with you—I am rarely quiet with you—because you rarely express anything to

me. I would be more quiet if you were less so
—less expressive if you were more so.

SHE *(pensively)*
The same old quarrel. Just the same for fif-
teen years! And all because you are you and
I am I! And I suppose it will go on forever—
I shall go on being silent, and you—

HE
I suppose I shall go on talking—but it really
doesn't matter—the silence or the talk—if we
had something to be silent about or to talk
about — something in common — that's the
point!

SHE
Do you really think we have nothing in com-
mon? We both like Dostoievsky and prefer
Burgundy to champagne.

HE
Our tastes and our vices are remarkably con-
genial, but our souls do not touch.

SHE
Our souls? Why should they? Every soul is
lonely.

HE
Yes, but doesn't want to be. The soul desires
to find something into which to fuse and so lose
its loneliness. This hope to lose the soul's loneliness by union—is love. It is the essence of
love as it is of religion.

SHE
Deacon, you are growing more holy every day.
You will drive me to drink.

HE *(moodily)*
    That will only complete the list.

SHE
    Well, then I suppose we may be more congenial
    —for in spite of what you say, our vices haven't
    exactly matched. You're ahead of me on the
    drink.

HE
    Yes, and you on some other things. But per-
    haps I can catch up, too—

SHE
    Perhaps—if you really give all your time to it,
    as you did last winter, for instance. But I
    doubt if I can ever equal your record in pota-
    tions.

HE *(bitterly)*
    I can never equal your record in the soul's in-
    fidelities.

SHE
    Well, do you expect my soul to be faithful
    when you keep hitting it with a gridiron?

HE
    No, I do not expect it of you! I have about
    given up the hope that you will ever respond
    either to my ideas about household and chil-
    dren or about our personal relations. You
    seem to want as little as possible of the things
    that I want much. I harass you by insisting.
    You anger and exasperate me by retreating.
    We were fools not to have separated long ago.

SHE
    Again! How you do repeat yourself, my
    dear!

HE

Yes, I am very weak. In spite of my better judgment I have loved you. But this time I mean it!

SHE

I don't believe you do. You never mean half the things you say.

HE

I do this time. This affair of yours with Hank is on my nerves. It is real spiritual infidelity. When you are interested in him you lose all interest in the household, the children and me. It is my duty to separate.

SHE

Oh, nonsense! I didn't separate from you when you were running after the widow last winter—spending hours with her every day, dining with her and leaving me alone, and telling me she was the only woman who had ever understood you.

HE

I didn't run after the widow, or any other woman except you. They ran after me.

SHE

Oh, of course! Just the same since Adam— not one of you has spirit enough to go after the apple himself! "They ran after you"—but you didn't run away very fast, did you?

HE

Why should I, when I wanted them to take possession if they could? I think I showed splendid spirit in running after you! Not more than a dozen other men have shown the same spirit. It is true, as you say, that other women understand and sympathize with me. They all do except you. I've never been able to be essentially unfaithfully, more's the pity. You are abler in that regard.

SHE

I don't think so. I may have liked other people, but I never dreamed of *marrying* anyone but *you*. . . . No, and I never thought any of them understood me, either. I took very good care they shouldn't.

SHE

Why, it was only the other day that you said Hank understood you better than I ever could. You said I was too virtuous, and that if I were worse you might see me!

SHE

As usual, you misquote me. What I said was that Hank and I were more alike, and that you are a virtuous stranger—a sort of wandering John the Baptist, preaching in the wilderness!

HE

Preachers don't do the things I do!

SHE

Oh, don't they?

HE

Well, I know I am as vicious as man can be. You would see that if you loved me. I am fully as bad as Hank.

SHE

Hank doesn't pretend to be virtuous, so perhaps you're worse. But I think you ought to make up your mind whether you're virtuous or vicious, and not assume to be both.

HE

I am both as a matter of fact, like everybody else. I am not a hypocrite. I love the virtuous and also the vicious. But I don't like to be left out in the cold when you are having an affair. When you are interested in the other, you are not in me.

SHE

Why do you pretend to fuss about lamps and such things when you are simply jealous? I call that hypocritical. I wish it were possible for a man to play fair. But what you want is to censor and control me, while you feel perfectly free to amuse yourself in every possible way.

HE

I am never jealous without cause, and you are. You object to my friendly and physical intimacies and then expect me not to be jealous of your soul's infidelities, when you lose all feeling for me. I am tired of it. It is a fundamental misunderstanding, and we ought to separate at once!

SHE

Oh, very well, if you're so keen on it. But remember, you suggest it. I never said I wanted to separate from you—if I had, I wouldn't be here now.

HE

No, because I've given all I had to you. I have nourished you with my love. You have harassed and destroyed me. I am no good because of you. You have made me work over you to the degree that I have no real life. You have enslaved me, and your method is cool aloofness. You want to keep on being cruel. You are the devil, who never really meant any harm, but who sneers at desires and never wants to satisfy. Let us separate—you are my only enemy!

SHE

Well, you know we are told to love our enemies.

HE

I have done my full duty in that respect. People we love are the only ones who can hurt us. They *are* our enemies, unless they love us in return.

SHE

"A man's enemies are those of his own household"—yes, especially if they love. You, on account of your love for me, have tyrannized over me, bothered me, badgered me, nagged me, for fifteen years. You have interfered with me, taken my time and strength, and prevented me from accomplishing great works for the good of humanity. You have crushed my soul, which longs for serenity and peace, with your perpetual complaining!

HE

Too bad. *(Indignantly)* Perpetual complaining!

SHE

Yes, of course. But you see, my dear, I am more philosophical than you, and I recognize all this as necessity. Men and women are natural enemies, like cat and dog—only more so. They are forced to live together for a time, or this wonderful race couldn't go on. In addition, in order to have the best children, men and women of totally opposed temperaments must live together. The shock and flame of two hostile temperaments meeting is what produces fine children. Well, we have fulfilled our fate and produced our children, and they are good ones. But really—to expect also to live in peace together—we as different as fire and water, or sea and land—that's too much!

HE

If your philosophy is correct, that is another argument for separation. If we have done our job together, let's go on our ways and try to do something else separately.

SHE

Perfectly logical. Perhaps it will be best. But no divorce—that's so commonplace.

HE

Almost as commonplace as your conventional attitude toward husbands—that they are necessarily uninteresting—*mon bete de mari*—as the typical Frenchwoman of fiction says. I find divorce no more commonplace than real infidelity.

SHE

Both are matters of every day. But I see no reason for divorce unless one of the spouses wants to marry again. I shall never divorce you. But men can always have children, and so they are perpetually under the sway of the great illusion. If you want to marry again, you can divorce me.

HE

As usual, you want to see me as a brute. I don't accept your philosophy. Children are the results of love, not because of it, and love should go on. It does go on, if once there has been the right relations. It is not re-marrying or the unconscious desire for further propagation that moves me—but the eternal need of that peculiar sympathy which has never been satisfied—to die without that is failure of what most appeals to the imagination of human beings.

SHE

But that *is* precisely the great illusion. That is the unattainable that lures us on, and that will lead you, I foresee, if you leave me, into the arms of some other woman.

HE

Illusion! Precisely what *is,* you call illusion. Only there do we find Truth. And certainly I *am* bitten badly with illusion or truth, whichever it is. It is Truth to me. But I fear it may be too late. I fear the other woman is impossible.

SHE *(pensively)*

"I cannot comprehend this wild swooning desire to wallow in unbridled unity." *(He makes angry gesture, she goes on quickly)* I was quoting your favorite philosopher. But as to being too late—no, no—you're more attractive than you ever were, and that shows your ingratitude to me, for I'm sure I have been a liberal education to you. You will easily find someone to adore you and console you for all your sufferings with me. But do be careful this time—get a good housekeeper.

HE

And *you* are more attractive than you ever were. I can see that others see that. I have been a liberal education to you, too.

SHE

Yes, a Pilgrim's Progress.

HE

I never would have seen woman, if I hadn't suffered you.

SHE

I never would have suffered man, if I hadn't seen you.

HE

You never saw me!

SHE

Alas—yes! *(With feeling)* I saw you as something very beautiful—very fine, sensitive —with more understanding than anyone I've ever known—more feeling—I still see you that way—but from a great—distance.

HE *(startled)*

Distance?

SHE

Yes. Don't you feel how far away from one another we are?

HE

I have felt it, as you know—more and more so—

132

that you were pushing me more and more away and seeking more and more somebody—something else. But this is the first time you have admitted feeling it.

SHE

Yes—I didn't want to admit it. But now I see it has gone very far. It is as though we were on opposite banks of a stream that grows wider —separating us more and more.

HE

Yes—

SHE

You have gone your own way, and I mine—and there is a gulf between us.

HE

Now you see what I mean—

SHE

Yes, that we ought to separate—that we *are* separated—and yet I love you.

HE

Two people may love intensely, and yet not be able to live together. It is too painful, for you, for me—

SHE

We have hurt one another too much—

HE

We have destroyed one another—we are enemies. *(Pause.)*

SHE

I don't understand it—how we have come to this—after our long life together. Have you forgotten all that? What wonderful companions we were? How gayly we took life with

133

both hands—how we played with it and with one another! At least, we have the past.

HE

The past is bitter—because the present is bitter.

SHE

You wrong the past.

HE

The past is always judged by the present. Dante said, the worst hell is in present misery to remember former happiness—

SHE

Dante was a man and a poet, and so ungrateful to life. *(Pause with feeling)* Our past to me is wonderful and will remain so, no matter what happens—full of color and life—complete!

HE

That is because our life together has been for you an episode.

SHE

No, it is because I take life as it is, not asking too much of it—not asking that any person or any relation be perfect. But you are an idealist —you can never be content with what it— You have the poison, the longing for perfection in your soul.

HE

No, not for perfection, but for union. That is not demanding the impossible. Many people have it who do not love as much as we do. No work of art is right, no matter how wonderful the material and the parts, if the whole, the unity, is not there.

SHE

That's just what I mean. You have wanted to treat our relation, and me, as clay, and model it into the form you saw in your imagination. You have been a passionate artist. But life is not a plastic material. *It* models us.

HE

You are right. I have had the egotism of the artist, directed to a material that cannot be formed. I must let go of you, and satisfy my need of union, of marriage, otherwise than with you.

SHE

Yes, but you cannot do that by seeking another woman. You would experience the same illusion—the same disillusion.

HE

How, then, can I satisfy this mystic need?

SHE

That is between you and your God—whom I know nothing about.

HE

If I could have stripped you of divinity and sought it elsewhere—in religion, in work—with the same intensity I sought it in you—we would not have needed this separation.

SHE

And we should have been very happy together!

HE

Yes—as interesting changers.

SHE

Exactly. The only sensible way for two fully grown people to be together—and that is won-

derful, too—think! To have lived together
for fifteen years and never to have bored one
another! To be still for one another the most
interesting persons in the world! How many
married people can say that? I've never *bored*
you, have I, Deacon?

HE

You have harassed, plagued, maddened, tor-
tured me! Bored me? No, never, you be-
witching devil! *(Moving toward her.)*

SHE

I've always adored the poet and mystic in you,
though you've almost driven me crazy, you
Man of God!

HE

I've always adored the woman in you, the mysterious, the beckoning and flying, that I cannot
possess!

SHE

Can't you forget God for a while, and come
away with me?

HE

Yes, darling; after all, you're one of God's
creatures!

SHE

Faithful to the end! A truce then, shall it be?
(Opening her arms) An armed truce?

HE

(seizing her) Yes, and in a trice! *(She
laughs.)*

[QUICK CURTAIN]

THE ANGEL INTRUDES

A COMEDY

By Floyd Dell

THE ANGEL INTRUDES

TIME—
The present

PLACE—THE PROLOGUE—
Washington Square, New York City

THE PLAY—
Jimmy Pendleton's Studio in Macdougal Alley

THE ANGEL INTRUDES was first produced by the Provincetown Players, on December 28, 1917, with the following cast:

A POLICEMAN, *Abram Gillette*
THE ANGEL, *James Light*
JIMMY PENDLETON, *Justus Sheffield*
ANNABELLE, *Edna St. Vincent Millay*

Scenes by Floyd Dell and Neal Reber. Directed by Nina Moise and Floyd Dell.

THE ANGEL INTRUDES
THE PROLOGUE

Washington Square by moonlight. A stream of Greenwich Villagers hurrying across to the Brevoort before the doors are locked. In their wake a sleepy policeman.

The Policeman stops suddenly on seeing an Angel with shining garments and great white wings, who has just appeared out of nowhere.

THE POLICEMAN

Hey, you!

THE ANGEL *(haughtily, turning)*

Sir! Are you addressing me?

THE POLICEMAN *(severely)*

Yes, an' I've a good mind to lock you up.

THE ANGEL *(surprised and indignant)*

How very inhospitable! Is that the way you treat strangers?

THE POLICEMAN

Don't you know it's agen the law of New York to parade the streets in a masquerade costume?

THE ANGEL

No; I didn't know. You see, I just arrived this minute from Heaven.

THE POLICEMAN

Ye look it. *(Taking his arm kindly)* See here, me lad, you've been drinkin' too many of them stingers. Ye'd better take a taxi and go home.

THE ANGEL

What! So soon?

THE POLICEMAN
> I know how ye feel. I've been that way meself.
> But I can't leave ye go trapesin' about in skirts.

THE ANGEL
> (*drawing away*) Sir, I am not trapesing about.
> I am attending to important business, and I
> must ask you not to detain me.

THE POLICEMAN (*suspiciously*)
> Not so fast, me laddie-buck. What business
> have you at this hour of the night? Tell me that!

THE ANGEL
> I don't mind telling you. It concerns a mortal
> called James Pendleton.

THE POLICEMAN
> (*genial again*) Aha! So you're a friend of
> Jimmy Pendleton's, are you?

THE ANGEL
> Not exactly. I am his Guardian Angel.

THE POLICEMAN
> Well, faith, he needs one! Come, me boy, I'll
> see ye safe to his door.

THE ANGEL
> Thank you. But, if you don't mind, I prefer
> to go alone. (*He turns away.*)

THE POLICEMAN
> Good-night to you, then. (*He idly watches the
> angelic figure walk away, and then stares with
> amazement as it spreads its wings and soars to
> the top of Washington Arch. Pausing there a
> moment, it soars again in the air, and is seen
> wafting its way over the neighboring housetops
> to the northeast. The Policeman shakes his
> head in disapproval.*)

THE PLAY

Jimmy Pendleton is dozing in an easy chair before the grate-fire in his studio in Washington Mews. A yellow-backed French novel has fallen from his knee to the floor. It is Anatole France's "La Revolte des Anges." A clock strikes somewhere. Jimmy Pendleton awakes.

JIMMY

What a queer dream! *(He looks at his watch)* One o'clock! The taxi ought to be here. *(He takes two steamship tickets from his pocket, looks at them, and puts them back. Then he commences to pace nervously up and down the room, muttering to himself)* Fool! Idiot! Imbecile! *(He is not, noticeably, any of these things; he is a very handsome man of forty. There is the blast of an auto horn outside. He makes an angry gesture)* Too late! That's the taxi. *(But he stands uncertainly in the middle of the floor. There is a hard pounding of the knocker)* Yes, yes! *(He makes a movement toward the door, when it suddenly opens, and a lovely lady enters. He stares at her in surprise)* Annabelle! *(Annabelle is little. Annabelle's petulant upturned lips are rosebud red. Annabelle's round eyes are baby-blue. Annabelle is—young.)*

ANNABELLE

Yes, it's me! *(There is a tiny lisp in Annabelle's speech)* I got tired of waiting, and the door was unlocked, so I came right in.

JIMMY
 Well!!

ANNABELLE *(hurt)*
 Aren't you glad to see me?

JIMMY
 I'm—delighted. But—but—I thought we were
 to meet at the pier!

ANNABELLE
 So we were.

JIMMY
 You haven't changed your mind?

ANNABELLE
 No...

JIMMY
 Er—good.

ANNABELLE
 But...

JIMMY
 Yes?...

ANNABELLE
 I got to wondering... *(Drifts to the easy chair
 in front of the fire.)*

JIMMY
 Wondering—about what? *(He looks at his
 watch.)*

ANNABELLE
 About love...

JIMMY
 Well... *(He lights a cigarette)* It's a subject
 that can stand a good deal of wondering about.
 I've wondered about it myself.

ANNABELLE
 That's just it—you speak so cynically about

it. I don't believe you're in love with me at
all!

JIMMY

Nonsense! Of course I'm in love with you.

ANNABELLE *(sadly)*

No, you're not.

JIMMY *(angrily)*

But, I tell you, I *am!*

ANNABELLE

No...

JIMMY

Foolish child!

ANNABELLE

Well, let's not quarrel about it now.

JIMMY *(vehemently)*

What do you suppose this insanity is if it isn't
love? What do you imagine leads me to this
preposterous elopement, if not that preposterous passion? What makes you come with
me in spite of the way I talk? Tell me that!

ANNABELLE

Perhaps I'm not coming.

JIMMY

Yes you are. It's foolish—mad—wicked—but
you're coming. *(She begins to cry softly)* If
not—ten minutes away is safety and peace and
comfort. Shall I call a taxi for you? *(She
shakes her head)* No; I thought not. Oh, it's
love all right.

ANNABELLE

I hate you!

JIMMY *(cheerfully)*

That's all right. *(Smiling)* I rather hate you

myself. And that's the final proof that this is love.

ANNABELLE *(sobbing)*
I thought love was something quite—different!

JIMMY
You thought it was beautiful. It isn't. It's just blithering, blathering folly. We'll both regret it to-morrow.

ANNABELLE
I won't!

JIMMY
Yes you will. It's human nature. Face the facts.

ANNABELLE *(tearfully)*
Facing the facts is one thing and being in love is another.

JIMMY
Quite so. Well, how long do you think your love for me will last?

ANNABELLE
Forever!

JIMMY
H-m! I predict that you will fall in love with the next man you meet.

ANNABELLE
I think you're perfectly horrid.

JIMMY
So do I. I disapprove of myself violently. I'm a doddering lunatic, incapable of thinking of anything but you. I can't work. I can't eat. I can't sleep. I'm no use to the world. I'm not a man—I'm a mess. I'm about to do something silly because I *can't* do anything else.

ANNABELLE *(pouting)*
   You've no respect for me.

JIMMY
   None whatever.   I love you.   And I'm going
   to carry you off.

ANNABELLE
   You're a brute.

JIMMY
   Absolutely.   I'd advise you to go straight home.

ANNABELLE *(defiantly)*
   Perhaps I shall!

JIMMY
   Then go quick.   *(He takes out his watch)*
   In one minute, if you are still here, I shall pick
   you up and carry you off to Italy.   Quick!
   There's the door!

ANNABELLE *(faintly)*
   I—I want to go...

JIMMY
   Well, why don't you?... Thirty seconds!

ANNABELLE
   I—I can't!

JIMMY
   (shutting his watch)   Time's up.   The die is
   cast!   *(He lifts her from the chair.   She clings
   to him helplessly)*   My darling!   My treasure!
   My beloved!—Idiot that I am!   *(He kisses her
   fiercely.)*

ANNABELLE
   (struggling in his arms)   No!   No!   No!
   Stop!

JIMMY
   Never!

10

ANNABELLE
Stop! Please! Please! Oh!... *(The light suddenly goes out, and an instant later blazes up again, revealing the Angel, who has suddenly arrived in the middle of the room. The two of them stare at the apparition.)*

THE ANGEL
I hope I am not intruding?

JIMMY
Why—why—not exactly!

THE ANGEL
If I am...

JIMMY
No, really...

ANNABELLE
(in his arms, indignantly) Jimmy! Who is that man?

JIMMY
(becoming aware of her and putting her down carefully) I—why—why, the fact is, I don't...

THE ANGEL
The fact is, madame, I am his Guardian Angel.

ANNABELLE
An Angel! Oh!

THE ANGEL
Tell me, *have* I intruded?

ANNABELLE
No; not at all!

THE ANGEL
Thank you for reassuring me. I feared for a moment that I had made an inopportune entrance. I was about to suggest that I with-

draw until you had finished the—er—ceremony
—which I seem to have interrupted.

JIMMY *(surprised)*

But wasn't that what you came for—to inter-
rupt?

THE ANGEL

I beg your pardon!

JIMMY *(bewilderedly)*

I mean—if you *are* my Guardian Angel, and
all that sort of thing, you *must* have come to
—to interfere!

THE ANGEL

I hope you will not think I would be capable of
such presumption!

JIMMY *(puzzled)*

You don't want to—so to speak—reform me?

THE ANGEL

Not at all. Why, I scarcely know you!

JIMMY

But you're my—my Guardian Angel, you say?

THE ANGEL

Ah, yes, to be sure. But the relation of an-
gelic guardianship has for some hundreds of
years been a purely nominal one. We have
come to feel that it is best to allow mortals to
attend to their own affairs.

JIMMY *(abruptly)*

Then, what *did* you come for?

THE ANGEL

For a change. One becomes tired of familiar
scenes. And I thought that perhaps my relationship to you might serve in lieu of an intro-
duction. I wanted to be among friends.

JIMMY
  Oh, I see.

ANNABELLE
  Of course. We're delighted to have you with
  us. Won't you sit down? *(She leads the way
  to the fire.)*

THE ANGEL
  (perching on the back of one of the big chairs)
  If you don't mind! My wings, you know.

JIMMY *(hesitantly)*
  Have a cigarette?

THE ANGEL
  Thank you. *(He takes one)* I am most
  anxious to learn the more important of your
  earthly arts and sciences. Please correct me
  if I go wrong. This is my first attempt, remember. *(He blows out a puff of smoke.)*

ANNABELLE
  (from the settle) You're doing it very nicely.

THE ANGEL
  It is incense to the mind.

ANNABELLE
  (laughingly, blowing a series of smoke rings)
  You must learn to do it like this!

THE ANGEL *(in awe)*
  That is too wonderful an art. I fear I can
  never learn it!

ANNABELLE
  I will teach you.

THE ANGEL *(earnestly)*
  If you were my teacher, I think I could learn
  anything.

ANNABELLE
  (*giggles, charmingly.*)
JIMMY (*embarrassed*)
  Really, Annabelle...
ANNABELLE
  What's the matter?
JIMMY
  Ordinarily I wouldn't mind you're flirting with
  strangers, but...
ANNABELLE (*indignantly*)
  Jimmy! How can you?
THE ANGEL
  It was my fault, I'm sure—if fault there was.
  But what is it—to flirt? You see, I wish to
  learn everything.
ANNABELLE
  I hope you never learn that.
THE ANGEL
  I put myself in your hands.
JIMMY
  Er—would you like a—drink?
THE ANGEL
  Thank you. I am very thirsty. (*Taking the
  glass*) This is very different from what we
  have in Heaven. (*He tastes it. A look of
  gratified surprise appears on his face*) And
  much better! (*He drains the glass and hands
  it back*) May I have some more?
ANNABELLE
  Be careful!
THE ANGEL
  What should I be careful of?

149

ANNABELLE

Don't take too much of that—if it's the first time.

THE ANGEL

Why not? It is an excellent drink.

JIMMY *(laughing)*

The maternal instinct! She is afraid you may make yourself—ridiculous.

THE ANGEL

Angels do not care for appearances. *(He stands up magnificently in the chair, towering above them)* Besides... *(Refilling his glass)* I feel that you do an injustice to this drink. Already it has made a new being of me. *(He looks at Annabelle)* I feel an emotion that I have never known before. If I were in Heaven, I should sing.

ANNABELLE

Oh! Won't you sing?

THE ANGEL

The fact is, I know nothing but hymns. And I'm tired of them. That was one reason why I left Heaven. And this robe... *(He stands up, viewing his garment with disapproval)* Have you an extra suit of clothes you could lend me?

JIMMY *(reflectively)*

Yes. I think I have some things that might fit. *(The Angel waits)* Do you want them now? I'll look. *(He goes into the bed-room. The Angel looks at Annabelle, until his gaze becomes insupportable and she covers her eyes. Then he comes over to her side.)*

THE ANGEL *(gravely)*
  I am very much afraid of you. *(He takes her hands in his.)*

ANNABELLE *(smiling)*
  One would never guess it!

THE ANGEL
  I am more afraid of you than I was of God. But even though I fear you, I must come close to you, and touch you. The strange, new emotion is like fire in my veins. This world has become beautiful to me because you are in it. I want to stay here so that I may be with you...

ANNABELLE
  (shaken, but doubting) For how long?

THE ANGEL
  Forever...

ANNABELLE
  (in his arms, surrendering to the word) Darling!

THE ANGEL
  I am *so* ignorant! There is something I want to do right now, only I do not know how to go about it properly. *(He bends shyly toward her lips.)*

ANNABELLE
  I will teach you. *(She kisses him.)*

THE ANGEL
  Heaven was nothing to this. *(They kiss again. Enter Jimmy, with an old suit of clothes over his arm. He pauses in dumbfounderment. At last he regains his voice.)*

JIMMY

Well! *(They look up. Neither of them is perturbed.)*

THE ANGEL *(blandly)*

Has something happened to annoy you? *(Jimmy shakes the clothes at him in an outraged gesture)* Oh, my new costume. Thank you so much! *(He takes them gratefully.)*

JIMMY

(bitterly, to Annabelle) I suppose I've no right to complain. You can make love to anybody you like. In fact, now that I come to think of it, I predicted this very thing. I said you'd fall in love with the next man you met. So it's off with the old love, and...

ANNABELLE *(calmly)*

I have never been in love before.

JIMMY

The fickleness of women is notorious. It is exceeded only by their mendacity. But Angels have up to this time stood in good repute. Your conduct, sir, is scandalous. I am amazed at you!

THE ANGEL

It may be scandalous, but it should not amaze you. It has happened too often before. I could quote you many texts from learned theological works. "And the sons of God looked at the daughters of men and saw that they were fair." But even if it were as unusual as you imagine, that would not deter me.

JIMMY

You are an unscrupulous wretch. If these are the manners of Heaven, I am glad it is so far away, and means of communication so difficult. A few more of you would corrupt the morals of five continents. You are utterly depraved— Here! What are you doing?

THE ANGEL

I am taking off my robes, so as to put on my new clothes.

JIMMY

Spare the common decencies at least. Go in the other room.

THE ANGEL

Certainly, if that is the custom here. *(With the clothes over his arm, he goes into the bedroom.)*

JIMMY *(sternly)*

And now tell me, what do you mean by this?

ANNABELLE *(simply)*

We are in love.

JIMMY

Do you mean to say you would throw me over for that fellow?

ANNABELLE

Why not?

JIMMY

What good is he? All he can do is sing hymns. In three months he'll be a tramp.

ANNABELLE

I don't care. And he won't be a tramp. I'll look after him.

JIMMY *(sneeringly)*

The maternal instinct! Well, take care of him if you like. But of course you know that in six weeks he'll fall in love with somebody else?

ANNABELLE

No he won't. I'm sure that I am the only girl in the world to him.

JIMMY

Of *course* you're the only girl in the world to him—now. You're the only one he's ever seen. But wait till he sees the others! Six weeks? On second thought I make it three days. Immortal love! *(He laughs.)*

ANNABELLE

What difference does it make? You don't understand. Whether it lasts a day or a year, while it lasts it will be immortal. *(The Angel enters, dressed in Jimmy's old clothes, and carrying his wings in his hands. He seems exhilarated.)*

THE ANGEL

How do I look?

JIMMY

It is customary to wear one's tie tucked inside the vest.

THE ANGEL

(flinging the ends of the gorgeous necktie over his shoulder) No! Though I have become a man, I do not without some regret put on the dull garb of mortality. I would not have my form lose all its original brightness. Even so it is the excess of glory obscured.

ANNABELLE

(coming over to him) You are quite right, darling. *(She tucks it inside his vest.)*

THE ANGEL

Thank you, beloved. And now these wings!

Take them, and burn them with your own sweet hands, so that I can never leave you, even if I would.

ANNABELLE

No! I would rather put them away for you in a closet, so that you can go and look at them any time you want to, and see that you have the means of freedom ready to your hand. I shall never hold you against your will. I do not want to burn your wings. I really don't! But if you insist... (*She takes the wings and approaches the grate.*)

JIMMY

(*to the Angel*) Don't let her do it! Fool! You don't know what you are doing. Listen to me! You think that she is wonderful—superior —divine. It is only natural. There are moments when I have thought so myself. But I know why I thought so, and you have yet to learn. Keep your wings, my friend, against the day of your awakening—the day when the glamour of sex has vanished, and you see in her, as you will see, an inferior being, with a weak body, a stunted mind, devoid of creative power, almost devoid of imagination, utterly lacking in critical capacity—a being who does not know how to work, nor how to talk, nor even how to play! (*Annabelle, putting down the wings beside the grate, stares at him in speechless anger.*)

THE ANGEL

Sir! Do you refer in those vulgar and insulting terms to the companion of my soul, the desire of my heart, the perfect lover whose lips have kindled my dull sense to ecstacy?

JIMMY

I do. Remember that I know her better than you do, young man. Take my advice and leave her alone. Even now it is not too late! Save yourself from this folly while there is time!

THE ANGEL

Never!

JIMMY

Then take these tickets, and I hope I never see either of you again! *(He holds out the tickets. Annabelle, after a pause, steps forward and takes them.)*

ANNABELLE

That is really sweet of you, Jimmy! *(The blast of an auto horn is heard outside.)*

JIMMY *(bitterly)*

And there's my taxi. Take that, too.

THE ANGEL

Farewell! *(He opens the door. Annabelle, at his side, turns and blows Jimmy a kiss. Stonily Jimmy watches them go out. Then he picks up his suitcase and goes, with an air of complete finality, into the other room. There is a moment's silence, and then the door opens softly, and the Angel looks in, enters surreptitiously, seizes up the wings, and with them safely clasped to his bosom, vanishes again through the door.)*

[CURTAIN]

BOUND EAST FOR CARDIFF

A PLAY

By Eugene G. O'Neill

Copyright, 19 ,
By Boni & Liveright, Inc.

All Rights Reserved

BOUND EAST FOR CARDIFF

As Produced at the Playwrights' Theater
New York City

YANK, *George Cram Cook*
DRISCOLL, *William Stuart*
COCKY, *Edward J. Ballantine*
DAVIS, *Harry Kemp*
SCOTTY, *Frank Shay*
OLESON, *B. J. O. Nordfeldt*
A NORWEGIAN, *Donald Corley*
SMITTY, *Lew Parrish*
IVAN, *Francis Buzzell*
THE CAPTAIN, *Henry Marion Hall*
THE SECOND MATE, *Eugene G. O'Neill*

BOUND EAST FOR CARDIFF

SCENE: *The seamen's forecastle on a British tramp steamer—an irregular-shaped compartment, the sides of which almost meet at the far end to form a triangle. Sleeping bunks about six feet long, ranged three deep, with a space of three feet separating the upper from the lower, are built against the sides. On the right above the bunks three or four port holes can be seen. In front of the bunks, rough, wooden benches. Over the bunks on the left, a lamp in a bracket. In the left foreground, a doorway. On the floor near it, a pail with a tin dipper. Oilskins are hanging from a hook near the doorway.*

The far side of the forecastle is so narrow that it contains only one series of bunks.

In under the bunks a glimpse can be had of sea-chests, suitcases, sea-boots, etc., jammed in indiscrimately.

At regular intervals of a minute or so the blast of the steamer's whistle can be heard above all the other sounds.

Five men are sitting on the benches talking. They are dressed in dirty, patched suits of dungaree, flannel shirts, and all are in their stocking feet. Four of the men are pulling on pipes and the air is heavy with rancid tobacco smoke. Sitting on the top bunk in the left foreground a

*blonde Norwegian is softly playing some folk
song on a battered accordion. He stops from
time to time to listen to the conversation.*

*In the lower bunk in the rear a dark-haired, mid-
dle-aged man is lying apparently asleep. One
of his arms is stretched limply over the side of
the bunk. His face is very pale and drops of
clammy perspiration glisten on his forehead.*

*It is nearing the end of the dog watch—about ten
minutes to eight in the evening.*

COCKY

*(a weazened runt of a man. He is telling a
story. The others are listening with amused,
incredulous faces, interrupting him at the end
of each sentence with loud, derisive guffaws)*
Maikin' love to me, she was! It's Gawd's
truth! A bloomin' nigger! Greased all over
with coconut oil, she was. Gawd blimey, I
couldn't stand 'er. Bloody old cow, I says;
and with that I fetched 'er a biff on the car wot
knocked 'er silly, an'—— *(He is interrupted by
a roar of laughter from the others.)*

DAVIS

*(a middle-aged man with brown hair and mus-
tache)* You're a liar, Cocky.

SCOTTY

(a dark young fellow) Ho-ho! Ye werr
neverr in New Guinea in yourr life, I'm thinkin'.

OLESON

(a Swede with an enormous blonde mustache—

160

with ponderous sarcasm) Yust tink of it! You
say she wass a cannibal, Cocky?

DRISCOLL

*(a red-haired giant with the battered features
of a prizefighter)* How cud ye doubt ut, Oleson? A quanc av the naygurs she musta been,
surely. Who else wud think herself aqual to
fallin' in love with a beauthiful, divil-may-care
rake av a man the loike av Cocky? *(A burst
of laughter from the crowd.)*

COCKY *(indignantly)*

Gawd strike me dead if it ain't true, every
bleedin' word of it. 'Appened ten year ago
come Christmas.

SCOTTY

'Twas a Christmas dinner she had her eyes on.

DAVIS

He'd a been a tough old bird.

DRISCOLL

'Tis lucky for both av ye ye escaped; for the
quane av the cannibal isles wad'a died av the
belly ache the day afther Christmas, divil a
doubt av ut. *(The laughter at this is long and
loud.)*

COCKY *(sullenly)*

Blarsted fat'eads! *(The sick man in the lower
bunk in the rear groans and moves restlessly.
There is a hushed silence. All the men turn
and stare at him.)*

DRISCOLL

Ssshh! *(In a hushed whisper)* We'd best not
be talkin' so loud and him tryin' to have a bit av
a sleep. *(He tiptoes softly to the side of the*

bunk) Yank! You'd be wantin' a drink av wather, maybe? *(Yank does not reply. Driscoll bends over and looks at him)* It's asleep he is, sure enough. His breath is chokin' in his throat loike wather gurglin' in a poipe. *(He comes back quietly and sits down. All are silent, avoiding each other's eyes.)*

COCKY

(after a pause) Pore devil! It's over the side for 'im, Gawd 'elp 'im.

DRISCOLL

Stop your croakin'! He's not dead yet and, praise God, he'll have many a long day yet before him.

SCOTTY

(shaking his head doubtfully) He's baad, mon, he's verry baad.

DAVIS

Lucky he's alive. Many a man's light woulda gone out after a fall like that.

OLESON

You saw him fall?

DAVIS

Right next to him. He and me was goin' down in Number Two hold to do some chippin'. He puts his leg over careless-like and misses the ladder and plumps straight down to the bottom. I was scared to look over for a minute, and then I heard him groan and I scuttled down after him. He was hurt bad inside, for the blood was drippin' from the side of his mouth. He was groanin' hard, but he never let a word out of him.

COCKY

An' you blokes remember when we 'auled 'im in 'ere? Oh 'ell, 'e says, oh 'ell—like that, and nothink else.

OLESON

Did the captain know where he iss hurted?

COCKY

That silly ol' josser! Wot the 'ell would 'e know abâht anythink?

SCOTTY (*scornfully*)

He fiddles in his mouth wi' a bit of glass.

DRISCOLL (*angrily*)

The divil's own life ut is to be out on the lonely sea wid nothin' betune you and a grave in the ocean, but a spindle-shanked, grey-whiskered auld fool the loike av him. 'Twas enough to make a saint shwear to see him wid his gold watch in his hand, tryin' to look as wise as an owl on a tree, and all the toime he not knowin' whether 'twas cholery or the barber's itch was the matther wid Yank.

SCOTTY (*sardonically*)

He gave him a dose of salts, na doot?

DRISCOLL

Divil a thing he gave him at all, but looked in the book he had wid him, and shook his head, and walked out widout sayin' a word, the second mate afther him no wiser than himself, God's curse on the two av thim!

COCKY

(*after a pause*) Yank was a good shipmate, pore beggar. Lent me four bob in Noo Yark, 'e did.

DRISCOLL *(warmly)*
   A good shipmate he was and is—none betther.
   Ye said no more than the truth, Cocky.   Five
   years and more ut is since first I shipped wid
   him, and we've stuck together iver since through
   good luck and bad.   Fights we've had, God
   help us, but 'twas only when we'd a bit av drink
   taken, and we always shook hands the nixt
   mornin'.   Whativer was his was mine, and
   many's the toime I'd a been on the beach or
   worse but for him.   And now—   *(His voice
   trembles as he fights to control his emotion)*
   Divil take me if I'm not startin' to blubber loike
   an auld woman, and he not dead at all, but
   goin' to live many a long year yet, maybe.

DAVIS
   The sleep'll do him good.   He seems better
   now.

OLESON
   If he wude eat something—

DRISCOLL
   Wud ye have him be eatin' in his condishun?
   Sure it's hard enough on the rest av us wid
   nothin' the matther wid our insides to be stom-
   achin' the skoff on this rusty lime-juicer.

SCOTTY *(indignantly)*
   It's a starvation ship.

DAVIS
   Plenty o' work and no food—and the owners
   ridin' around in carriages!

OLESON
   Hash, hash!   Stew, stew!   Marmalade, py
   damn!   *(He spits disgustedly.)*

COCKY

Bloody swill! Fit only for swine is wot I say.

DRISCOLL

And the dishwather they disguise wid the name av tea! And the putty they call bread! My belly feels loike I'd swalleyed a dozen rivets at the thought av ut! And sea-biscuit that'd break the teeth av a lion if he had the misfortune to take a bite at one! *(Unconsciously they have all raised their voices, forgetting the sick man in their sailor's delight at finding something to grumble about.)*

THE NORWEGIAN

(stops playing accordion—says slowly) And rot-ten po-tay-toes! *(He starts in playing again. The sick man gives a groan of pain.)*

DRISCOLL

(holding up his hand) Shut your mouths, all av you. 'Tis a hell av a thing for us to be complainin' about our guts, and a sick man maybe dyin' listenin' to us. *(Gets up and shakes his fist at the Norwegian)* God stiffen you, ye square-head scut! Put down that organ av yours or I'll break your ugly face for you. Is that banshee schreechin' fit music for a sick man? *(The Norwegian puts his accordion in the bunk and lays back and closes his eyes. Driscoll goes over and stands beside Yank. The steamer's whistle sounds particularly loud in the silence.)*

DAVIS

Damn this fog! *(Reaches in under a bunk and yanks out a pair of seaboots which he pulls on)*

My lookout next, too. Must be nearly eight bells, boys. *(With the exception of Oleson, all the men sitting up put on oilskins, sou' westers, seaboots, etc., in preparation for the watch on deck. Oleson crawls into a lower bunk on the right.)*

SCOTTY

My wheel.

OLESON *(disgustedly)*

Nothin' but yust dirty weather all dis voyage. I yust can't sleep when weestle blow. *(He turns his back to the light and is soon fast asleep and snoring.)*

SCOTTY

If this fog keeps up, I'm tellin' ye, we'll no be in Cardiff for a week or more.

DRISCOLL

'Twas just such a night as this the auld Dover wint down. Just about this toime it was, too, and we all sittin' round in the fo'castle, Yank beside me, whin all av a suddint we heard a great slitherin' crash, and the ship heeled over til we was all in a heap on wan side. What came afther I disremimber exactly, except 'twas a hard shift to get the boats over the side before the auld teakittle sank. Yank was in the same boat wid me, and sivin morthal days we drifted wid scarcely a drop of wather or a bite to chew on. T'was Yank here that held me down whin I wanted to jump into the ocean, roarin' mad wid the thirst. Picked up we were on the same day wid only Yank in his senses, and him steerin' the boat.

COCKY *(protestingly)*

Blimey, but you're a cheerful blighter, Driscoll! Talkin' abaht shipwrecks in this 'ere blushin' fog. *(Yank groans and stirs uneasily, opening his eyes. Driscoll hurries to his side.)*

DRISCOLL

Are you feelin' any betther, Yank?

YANK

(in a weak voice) No.

DRISCOLL

Sure you must be. You look as sthrong as an ox. *(Appealing to the others)* Am I tellin' him a lie?

DAVIS

The sleep's done you good.

COCKY

You'll be 'avin' your pint of beer in Cardiff this day week.

SCOTTY

And fish and chips, mon!

YANK *(peevishly)*

What're yuh all liein' fur? D'yuh think I'm scared to— *(He hesitates as if frightened by the word he is about to say.)*

DRISCOLL

Don't be thinkin' such things! *(The ship's bell is heard heavily tolling eight times. From the forecastle head above, the voice of the lookout rises in a long wail: Aaalls well. The men look uncertainly at Yank as if undecided whether to say good-bye or not.)*

YANK

(in an agony of fear) Don't leave me, Drisc!

167

I'm dyin', I tell yuh. I won't stay here alone with everyone snorin'. I'll go out on deck. (*He makes a feeble attempt to rise, but sinks back with a sharp groan. His breath comes in wheezy gasps*) Don't leave me, Drisc! (*His face grows white and his head falls back with a jerk.*)

DRISCOLL

Don't be worryin', Yank. I'll not move a step out av here—and let that divil av a bosun curse his black head off. You speak a word to the bosun, Cocky. Tell him that Yank is bad took and I'll be stayin' wid him a while yet.

COCKY

Right-o. (*Cocky, Davis, and Scotty go out quietly.*)

COCKY

(*from the alleyway*) Gawd blimey, the fog's thick as soup.

DRISCOLL

Are ye satisfied now, Yank? (*Receiving no answer, he bends over the still form*) He's fainted, God help him! (*He gets a tin dipper from the bucket, and bathes Yank's forehead with the water. Yank shudders and opens his eyes.*)

YANK (*slowly*)

I thought I was goin' then. Wha' did yuh wanta wake me up fur?

DRISCOLL (*with forced gaiety*)

Is it wishful for heaven ye are?

YANK (*gloomily*)

Hell, I guess.

DRISCOLL

(crossing himself involuntarily) For the love av the saints, don't be talkin' loike that! You'd give a man the creeps. It's chippin' rust on deck you'll be in a day or two wid the best av us. *(Yank does not answer, but closes his eyes wearily. The seaman who has been on lookout, a young Englishman, comes in and takes off his dripping oilskins. While he is doing this the man whose turn at the wheel has been relieved enters. He is a dark, burly fellow with a round, stupid face. The Englishman steps softly over to Driscoll. The other crawls into a lower bunk.)*

THE ENGLISHMAN *(whispering)*

How's Yank?

DRISCOLL

Betther. Ask him yourself. He's awake.

YANK

I'm all right, Smitty.

SMITTY

Glad to hear it, Yank. *(He crawls to an upper bunk and is soon asleep. The stupid-faced seaman who came in after Smitty twists his head in the direction of the sick man)* You feel gude, Jank?

YANK *(wearily)*

Yes, Ivan.

IVAN

Dot's gude. *(He rolls over on his side and falls asleep immediately.)*

YANK

(after a pause, broken only by snores—with a

169

bitter laugh) Good-bye and good luck to the lot of you!

DRISCOLL

Is ut painin' you again?

YANK

It hurts like hell—here. *(He points to the lower part of his chest on the left side)* I guess my old pump's busted. Ooohh! *(A spasm of pain contracts his pale features. He presses his hand to his side and writhes on the thin mattress of his bunk. The perspiration stands out in beads on his forehead.)*

DRISCOLL *(terrified)*

Yank! Yank! What is ut? *(Jumping to his feet)* I'll run for the captain. *(He starts for the doorway.)*

YANK

(sitting up in his bunk, frantic with fear) Don't leave me, Drisc! For God's sake, don't leave me alone! *(He leans over the side of his bunk and spits. Driscoll comes back to him)* Blood! Ugh!

DRISCOLL

Blood again! I'd best be gettin' the captain.

YANK

No, no, don't leave me! If yuh do I'll git up and follow yuh. I ain't no coward, but I'm scared to stay here with all of them asleep and snorin'. *(Driscoll, not knowing what to do, sits down on the bench beside him. He grows calmer and sinks back on the mattress)* The captain can't do me no good—yuh know it yourself. The pain ain't so bad now, but I thought

it had me then.   It was like a buzz-saw cuttin'
into me.

DRISCOLL *(fiercely)*
God blarst ut! *(The captain and the second
mate of the steamer enter the forecastle. The
captain is an old man with grey mustache and
whiskers. The mate is clean shaven and middle-aged. Both are dressed in simple blue uni-
forms.)*

THE CAPTAIN
(taking out his watch and feeling Yank's pulse)
And how is the sick man?

YANK *(feebly)*
All right, sir.

THE CAPTAIN
And the pain in the chest?

YANK
It still hurts, sir; worse than ever.

THE CAPTAIN
*(taking a thermometer from his pocket and
putting it in Yank's mouth)* Here, be sure and
keep this in under your tongue—not over it.

THE MATE
(after a pause) Isn't this your watch on deck,
Driscoll?

DRISCOLL
Yes, sorr; but Yank was fearin' to be alone,
and—

THE CAPTAIN
That's all right, Driscoll.

DRISCOLL
Thank ye, sorr.

THE CAPTAIN

(stares at his watch for a moment or so; then takes the thermometer from Yank's mouth and goes to the lamp to read it. His expression grows very grave. He beckons the mate and Driscoll to the corner near the doorway. Yank watches them furtively. The captain speaks in a low voice to the mate) Way up, both of them. *(To Driscoll)* Has he been spitting blood again?

DRISCOLL

Not much for the hour just past, sorr; but before that—

THE CAPTAIN

A great deal?

DRISCOLL

Yes, sorr.

THE CAPTAIN

He hasn't eaten anything?

DRISCOLL

No, sorr.

THE CAPTAIN

Did he drink that medicine I sent him?

DRISCOLL

Yes, sorr; but it didn't stay down.

THE CAPTAIN

(shaking his head) I'm afraid—he's very weak. I can't do anything else for him. It's too serious for me. If this had only happened a week later we'd be in Cardiff in time to—

DRISCOLL

Plaze help him someway, sorr!

THE CAPTAIN *(impatiently)*

But, my good man, I'm not a doctor. *(More kindly as he sees Driscoll's grief)* You and he have been shipmates a long time?

DRISCOLL

Five years and more, sorr.

THE CAPTAIN

I see. Well, don't let him move. Keep him quiet and we'll hope for the best. I'll read the matter up and send him some medicine—something to ease the pain, anyway. *(Goes over to Yank)* Keep up your courage. You'll be better to-morrow. *(He breaks down lamely before Yank's steady gaze)* We'll pull you through all right—and—hm—well—coming, Robinson? Dammit! *(He goes out hurriedly, followed by the mate.)*

DRISCOLL

(trying to conceal his anxiety) Didn't I tell you you wasn't half as sick as you thought you was. The captain'll have you on deck cursin' and swearin' loike a trooper before the week is out.

YANK

Don't lie, Drisc. I heard what he said, and if I didn't I c'd tell by the way I feel. I know what's goin' to happen. I'm going to— *(He hesitates for a second—then resolutely)* I'm goin' to die, that's what, and the sooner the better!

DRISCOLL *(wildly)*

No, and be damned to you, you're not. I'll not let you.

YANK

It ain't no use, Drisc. I ain't got a chance; but I ain't scared. Gimme a drink of water, will yuh, Drisc? My throat's burnin' up. *(Driscoll brings the dipper full of water and supports his head while he drinks in great gulps.)*

DRISCOLL

(seeking vainly for some word of comfort) Are ye feelin' more aisy-loike now?

YANK

Yes—now—when I know it's all up. *(A pause)* You mustn't take it so hard, Drisc. I was just thinkin' it ain't as bad as people think—dyin'. I ain't never took much stock in the truck them sky-pilots preach. I ain't never had religion; but I know whatever it is what comes after it can't be no worser'n this. I don't like to leave you, Drisc, but—that's all.

DRISCOLL

(with a groan) Lad, lad, don't be talkin'!

YANK

This sailor life ain't much to cry about leavin' —just one ship after another—hard work, small pay, and bum grub; and when we git into port, just a drunk, endin' up in a fight, and all your money gone, and then ship away again. Never meetin' no nice people; never gittin' outa sailor town, hardly, in any port; travelin' all over the world and never seein' none of it; without no one to care whether you're alive or dead. *(With a bitter smile)* There ain't much in all that that'd make yuh sorry to lose it, Drisc.

DRISCOLL *(gloomily)*

It's a hell av a life—the sea.

YANK (*musingly*)

It must be great to stay on dry land all your life and have a farm, with a house of your own, with cows and pigs and chickens, way in the middle of the land where yuh'd never smell the sea or see a ship. It must be great to have a wife, and kids to play with at night after supper when your work is done. It must be great to have a home of your own, Drisc.

DRISCOLL

(*with a great sigh*) It must, surely; but what's the use av thinkin' av ut? Such things are not for the loikes av us.

YANK

Sea-farin' is all right when you're young and don't care; but we ain't chickens no more, and somehow, I dunno, this last year has seemed rotten, and I've had a hunch I'd quit—with you, of course—and we'd save our coin, and go to Canada or Argentine or some place and git a farm, just a small one, just enough to live on. I never told yuh this 'cause I thought yuh'd laugh at me.

DRISCOLL (*enthusiastically*)

Laugh at you, is ut? When I'm havin' the same thoughts myself, toime afther toime. It's a grand idea, and we'll be doin' ut sure if you'll stop your crazy notions—about—about bein' so sick.

YANK (*sadly*)

Too late. We shouldn't a made this trip, and, then— How'd all the fog git in here?

DRISCOLL

Fog?

YANK

Everythin' looks misty. Must be my eyes git-
tin' weak, I guess. What was we talkin' of a
minute ago? Oh yes, a farm. It's too late.
(*His mind wandering*) Argentine, did I say?
D'yuh remember the times we've had in Buenos
Aires? The moving pictures in Barracas?
Some class to them, d'yuh remember?

DRISCOLL

(*with satisfaction*) I do that; and so does the
piany player. He'll not be forgettin' the black
eye I gave him in a hurry.

YANK

Remember the time we was there on the beach
and had to go to Tommy Moore's boarding-
house to git shipped? And he sold us rotten
oilskins and seaboots full of holes, and shipped
us on a skysail yarder round the Horn, and
took two months' pay for it! And the days
we used to sit on the park benches along the
Paseo Colon with the vigilantes lookin' hard at
us! And the songs at the Sailor's Opera, where
the guy played ragtime—d'yuh remember them?

DRISCOLL

I do, surely.

YANK

And La Plata—phew, the stink of the hides!
I always liked Argentine—all except that booze,
caña. How drunk we used to git on that, remember?

DRISCOLL

Cud I forget ut? My head pains me at the
menshun av that divil's brew.

YANK

Remember the night I went crazy with the heat in Singapore? And the time you was pinched by the cops in Port Said? And the time we was both locked up in Sydney for fightin'?

DRISCOLL

I do so.

YANK

And that fight on the dock at Cape Town. (*His voice betrays great inward perturbation.*)

DRISCOLL (*hastily*)

Don't be thinkin' av that now. 'Tis past and gone.

YANK

D'yuh think He'll hold it up against me?

DRISCOLL (*mystified*)

Who's that?

YANK

God. They say He sees everything. He must know it was done in fair fight—in self-defense —don't yuh think?

DRISCOLL

Av course. Ye stabbed him, and be damned to him, for the skulkin' swine he was, afther him tryin' to stick you in the back, and you not suspectin'. Let your conscience be aisy. I wisht I had nothin' blacker than that on my sowl. I'd not be afraid av the angel Gabriel himself.

YANK

(*with a shudder*) I c'd see him a minute ago with the blood spurtin' out of his neck. Ugh!

12

DRISCOLL

The fever, ut is, that makes you see such things. Give no heed to ut.

YANK *(uncertainly)*

You dont think' He'll hold it up agin me—God, I mean?

DRISCOLL

If there's justice in hiven, no! *(Yank seems comforted by this assurance.)*

YANK

(after a pause) We won't reach Cardiff for a week at least. I'll be buried at sea.

DRISCOLL

(putting his hands over his ears) Ssshh! I won't listen to you.

YANK

(as if he had not heard him) It's as good a place as any other, I s'pose—only I always wanted to be buried on dry land. But what the hell'll I care—then? *(Fretfully)* Why should it be a rotten night like this, with that damned whistle blowin' and people snorin' all around? I wish the stars was out, and the moon, too; I c'd lie out on deck and look at them, and it'd make it easier to go—somehow.

DRISCOLL

For the love av God, don't be talkin' loike that!

YANK

Whatever pay's comin' to me yuh can divvy up with the rest of the boys; and you take my watch. It ain't worth much, but it's all I've got.

DRISCOLL

But have ye no relations at all to call your own?

YANK

No, not as I know of. One thing I forgot: You know Fanny, the barmaid, at the Red Stork in Cardiff?

DRISCOLL

Sure and who doesn't?

YANK

She's been good to me. She tried to lend me half a crown when I was broke there last trip. Buy her the biggest box of candy yuh c'n find in Cardiff. *(Breaking down—in a choking voice)* It's hard to ship on this voyage I'm goin' on—alone! *(Driscoll reaches out and grasps his hand. There is a pause, during which both fight to control themselves)* My throat's like a furnace. *(He gasps for air)* Gimme a drink of water, will yuh, Drisc? *(Driscoll gets him a dipper of water)* I wish this was a pint of beer. Oooohh! *(He chokes, his face convulsed with agony, his hands tearing at his shirt front. The dipper falls from his nerveless fingers.)*

DRISCOLL

For the love av God, what is ut, Yank?

YANK

(speaking with tremendous difficulty) S'long, Drisc! *(He stares straight in front of him with eyes starting from their sockets)* Who's that?

DRISCOLL

Who? What?

YANK *(faintly)*

A pretty lady dressed in black. *(His face*

*twitches and his body writhes in a final spasm,
then straightens out rigidly.)*

DRISCOLL

(pale with horror) Yank! Yank! Say a word
to me, for the love av hiven! *(He shrinks
away from the bunk, making the sign of the
cross. Then comes back and puts a trembling
hand on Yank's chest and bends closely over
the body.)*
Cocky's voice *(from the alleyway)* Oh, Driscoll! Can you leave Yank for arf a mo and
give me a 'and?

DRISCOLL

(with a great sob) Yank! *(He sinks down
on his knees beside the bunk, his head on his
hands. His lips move in some half-remembered
prayer.)*

COCKY

*(Enters, his oilskins and sou'wester glistening
with drops of water)* The fog's lifted. *(Cocky
sees Driscoll and stands staring at him with
open mouth. Driscoll makes the sign of the
cross again.)*

COCKY *(mockingly)*

Sayin' 'is prayers! *(He catches sight of the
still figure in the bunk and an expression of
awed understanding comes over his face. He
takes off his dripping sou'wester and stands
scratching his head.)*

COCKY

(in a hushed whisper) Gawd blimey.

[CURTAIN]

180

THE WIDOW'S VEIL

A COMEDY

By Alice Rostetter

CHARACTERS

KATY MACMANUS (she's young and married),
MRS. PHELAN, her neighbor, to your left.
VOICES AND OTHER SOUNDS,
TIME—Twenty-four hours and not so long ago.
PLACE—The meeting place of tender-hearted
women. The floor's the fifth.

THE WIDOW'S VEIL was first produced by the
Provincetown Players at the Playwrights' Theater, New York, on January 17, 1919, with the
following cast:

KATY MACMANUS (she's young and married),
                                    Mary Payne
Her Neighbor, MRS. PHELAN, to your left,
                                    Alice Rostetter
VOICES AND OTHER SOUNDS,
                            Lewis B. Ell and Others
Directed by George Cram Cook

THE WIDOW'S VEIL

The curtain rises on a dumb-waiter shaft. Rear,
stands the opposite wall, the bricks worn a gray
drab in the cracks. There's the rope in the cen-
ter and the side ropes are vibrating still. The
closed doors into the kitchens, right and left,
are seen and there's silence on the two sides.
The doors into the kitchens on the floors above
and below cannot be seen, but the sounds ema-
nating from them are distinguishable. From
the floor above, the sixth floor left, comes muf-
fled the crying of an irritable baby, and from
the cellar comes a voice, bad-tempered and with
an edge on it. 'Tis the voice—the official voice
—of the Janitor.

VOICE OF JANITOR
   Garbage! *(The two kitchen doors on the floor*
   below, the fourth floor, promptly open with two
   clicks, the two pails are slammed on and the
   two doors shut. The Janitor is heard whipping
   down the dumb-waiter, dumping the two cans
   empty, replacing them, giving two of the short-
   est whistles. Then the dumb-waiter is whipped
   up; the two doors opened, the two pails taken
   off. The dumb-waiter appears at stage level,
   the fifth floor, and the two whistles shrill right
   and left. A careful step is heard and Mrs.
   Phelan opens the door.)

183

MRS. PHELAN

Good-mornin', Mr. Kelly.

VOICE OF JANITOR

Garbage! *(He blows, sharper than ever, the whistle of the kitchen, right. Mrs. Phelan is heard putting on her light pail. The dumbwaiter is whipped out of sight. Mrs. Phelan is revealed from the waist up; the merest glimpse of a kitchen wall and corner of a nearby table can be seen. Mrs. Phelan is very neat and in dull-colored clothes. The hope-of-better-things-turning-up never smiled from her face. Her hair is graying and drab-colored. She leans out and talks down.)*

MRS. PHELAN

I'll be takin' her milk off, Mr. Kelly. She's maybe sleepin'—or readin'—or— *(She leans across and knocks on the door; no one comes. The whistle, left, blows; the waiter shoots up. Mrs. Phelan takes off her pail and her neighbor's milk and bread. As the waiter shoots up to the floor above she is seen disappearing and her door slipping shut. On the sixth floor the two whistles blow and the two doors are opened and the crying of the baby comes down from the edge of the kitchen door, left.)*

VOICE OF WOMAN SIXTH FLOOR RIGHT

(an easy, young voice and cheerful) Good-mornin', Mrs. Tynan, and how's the little one to-day?

VOICE OF WOMAN SIXTH FLOOR LEFT

(a sarcastic voice made bitter by lack of sleep) Ye can hear how, can't ye? Not a thing the

matter with him save his father's bad temper.
(She slams on her pail, punctuating her belief)
And I'll get that out of him, if I haf to— *(The
door left slams shut.)*

VOICE OF WOMAN SIXTH FLOOR RIGHT
(talking back into the room) And did you hear
that, Maggie! *(She puts on her pail; then, as
the vibrating ropes jerk tight, comes a sharp
but polite)* Can't you wait, Mr. Kelly? I've
more for you. *(Slightly fainter, but distinct,
as she bends to lift her package)* And, Maggie, that's married bliss for you. It's us old
maids *(strong, as she puts on the package)* is
the lucky ones *(the dumb-waiter flies down)*
believe me! *(Her door shuts. The pails are
slammed back, the waiter flies past and up, the
two whistles shrill and the cellar door bangs
shut. The door, sixth floor left, opens, the
baby squalling clear again; the pail snatched
off and the door shut. The door, sixth floor
right, opens.)*

VOICE OF WOMAN SIXTH FLOOR RIGHT
*(as she removes pail and with politic smooth-
ness, calling down)* Mr. Kelly, will you be
doin' me a small favor? *(Silence)* Mr. Kelly!
(with sincerity) The old crank! *(The door
is slammed shut. Silence. The wind makes a
faint, mournful sound up the shaft. A voice
from the floor below is heard humming a bit of
happy song. The wind again keens faint. Mrs.
Phelan opens her door, left, leans across and
listens. There's no sound. She leans further
out. After a second more she knocks, clear and*

*determined. A step is heard. She knocks
again. The door, right, opens slow.)*

MRS. PHELAN

Good-mornin', Mrs. MacManus! *(Mrs. Mac-
Manus looks out. Ah, but she's young and
pretty! The red hair on her is bright and warm
as a flame; the white skin on her, soft. But
she's pale and tired now and her two eyes have
been weeping. She's on a blue kimono of the
shade of her eyes when they're glad. Her de-
pressed manner warms up with a flick of im-
patience as she answers.)*

MRS. MACMANUS

Ah, it's you that can say good-mornin', Mrs.
Phelan, and no troubles at all.

MRS. PHELAN

(with pleasurable, but restrained, anticipation)
And is it trouble ye have?

MRS. MACMANUS

(the gulp in her voice now) Me man's wurse!

MRS. PHELAN

Wurse? And me not knowin' he was sick!
*(Mrs. MacManus nods, biting her red lips to
keep the weeping back)* Poor soul! poor soul!
But the good Lord will be helpin' ye, Mrs. Mac-
Manus. He—

MRS. MACMANUS

(sharp again) I'm not doubtin' that, Mrs.
Phelan, and me as good a Catholic as y'rself.
(Her lips are at it again) But— Oh—oh—
Mrs. Phelan, he's goin' on me!

MRS. PHELAN

Goin'? Houly Mary, is it dyin' ye mean?

THE WIDOW'S VEIL

(Mrs. MacManus, with a nod and a loud ketch in her voice, begins to sob) There, there, now! Ye poor young thing! And me seein' him only yisterday buyin' the mornin' eggs for ye. Ttt-ttt! And him so hale and hearty—seemin'.

MRS. MACMANUS

'Twas near night he was taken. Ah— *(In a burst of nervous, strained energy)* Mrs. Phelan, the horror is on me still, and me sittin' quiet and lone the night through!

MRS. PHELAN

(visibly cheering) Ah, be tellin' me all, Mrs. MacManus. 'Twill ease the heart of ye. *(Briskly, working in her métier, gossip)* Let you bring up a chair and be kneelin' comfortable. *(Mrs. MacManus nods. They disappear, Mrs. Phelan reappearing first and fixing herself for a long talk. She shakes her head with the long sorrow, like a healthy person at a wake. She raises her hands in rich despair. Mrs. MacManus reappears, arranging a bright shawl carefully over her shoulders; she drapes it over her shoulders, her features both woebegone and interested in the hanging of the goods.)*

MRS. PHELAN

(a little impatient) It hangs fine, Mrs. MacManus. Be tellin' me all! 'Twill ease y'r heart. *(Mrs. MacManus leans, graceful and tired)* Begin at the beginnin'.

MRS. MACMANUS

(the heartache in her voice) Himself came home yester e'en and the clock at four.

187

MRS. PHELAN
At four! Was he red?

MRS. MACMANUS *(careful)*
Not at four. He was white like—like—

MRS. PHELAN
(nodding, understanding) The bit stone at the head of a gra—

MRS. MACMANUS
And the blood all gone from his face, Mrs. Phelan.

MRS. PHELAN
(nodding, fatal) 'Twas them chills.

MRS. MACMANUS
And his hand cold—cold as the hand of a marble saint.

MRS. PHELAN
Ye don't say that!

MRS. MACMANUS
And he'd the pain in his head and the throat of him burnin' like hot peat.

MRS. PHELAN
Ah, now, now! Ah, 'tis true, Mrs. MacManus, in the midst of life we're in death. And what's the doctor namin' it?

MRS. MACMANUS
And would he let a doctor in the house, and me beggin' him one hour by the clock and the tears in me eyes!

MRS. PHELAN
Ah, ye should not be askin' him, ye poor young bride. Just have the man in. I'll step around meself and be askin' the doctor to have a look in.

MRS. MACMANUS

Ye're kind, Mrs. Phelan.

MRS. PHELAN

Not at all. But I'm feerin' it's too late. Them chills is— *(Mrs. MacManus breaks down and sobs)* There, there, now, dearie— *(She pats her across the shaft, forcing hope, to be kind)* It—maybe it's only a germ it is, and them that thick in the street. *(Mrs. MacManus sobs the harder)* Now, now, ye'll blubber all the pretty out of y'r face. *(Mrs. MacManus fumbles about for a handkerchief)* Is it a hangkercheef ye want? *(She extracts one from her apron belt)* Me cousin's after leavin' it here *(she examines the border)* on the way home from Mr. Reilly's wake. *(She passes it across)* Ye'll not mind the black border, I hope? *(Mrs. MacManus, grasping it, sobs violently, like a child)* Ah, now, don't take on. It's not stretched out he is yet. Not yet, dearie. Not yet. Be tellin' me more and ease y'r heart. *(She sums up brightly)* He came home at four and the hand of him all like the hand of a corpse. Ttt, ttt! And straight he wint for the bed. And then?

MRS. MACMANUS

(sobbing more quietly) He wouldn't eat the meat I was fixin', the way he likes, with me own two hands. And at nine by the clock he starts mutterin' and tossin' and twistin' like a soul in the black depths of hell. And— *(She looks up)* I takes a chair and I sits beside him and I tries catchin' hold of his hand and kissin' it,

the way he'll be always doin' and him in his health. And— *(A bright spark of anger lights up her eye)* Ye'll not believe what I'm tellin' ye, Mrs. Phelan!

MRS. PHELAN
(nodding affirmation) Go on, Mrs. Mac-Manus.

MRS. MACMANUS
What does he do but snatch back his hand and curses like the mad king of Kildare. And me —and me— *(She resumes a gentle weeping.)*

MRS. PHELAN *(solemnly)*
A ten-day bride! Go on, Mrs. MacManus.

MRS. MACMANUS
(a little indistinctly) And, says he, shoutin': "Can't ye be leavin' me to die in peace—for one moment!" Oh, Mrs. Phelan, the red face of him, and his eyes closed in it.

MRS. PHELAN
(recording the change) 'Twas red by that— in spots?

MRS. MACMANUS
No, just plain. And me watchin' it the clock 'round.

MRS. PHELAN
(again summing up) Red—and hot—and his mind bad. Poor young thing! Poor young thing! But go on, while ye can.

MRS. MACMANUS
And when the cold mornin' light comes stralin' in, and the clock at four, he stops mutterin' and tossin', and lies still, except for the sound in his throat.

MRS. PHELAN

Glory be to God, Mrs. MacManus, it's the end! It's the rattl—

MRS. MACMANUS *(alarmed)*

What d'ye mean, Mrs. Phelan?

MRS. PHELAN

(rapidly easing her own heart and keeping the raw truth, as she sees it, from Mrs. MacManus) Ye'll be knowin' soon enough. Arra, arra, it's the like of that hangkercheef ye'll be usin' soon. But go on, Mrs. MacManus, go on. Ah, it's the night ye had!

MRS. MACMANUS

(looking at her for further comfort) And sittin' on me chair, thinkin', it comes to me sudden and quick 'twas warnin' me Pat was, Sunday night last.

MRS. PHELAN

Warnin' ye?

MRS. MACMANUS

I'm knowin' now he had a presintement of what was to come. Says he—the night of Sunday—ye know his bright way—says he: "Katy, if I go to join the angels afore you do—"

MRS. PHELAN

Sakes!

MRS. MACMANUS

"—ye must be marryin' again. Ye're too pretty to be livin' alone, though," says he, smilin', "the widow's veil will become ye fine, and that hair warmin' the heart of a man. It'll set ye fine, Katy."

MRS. PHELAN

It will. Ye've a black skirt? *(Mrs. Mac-
Manus gives a cry, all tears and despair, and a
bit of protest. Mrs. Phelan speaks sternly)*
Ye must be ready, out of respect for the good
man. Have ye a waist will do?

MRS. MACMANUS

(muffled, patient, despairing) Me new one
with the gold lace and—

MRS. PHELAN

(nodding, business-like) The little vest! 'Twill
do fine and easy fixed. Have ye a bit of bonnet?

MRS. MACMANUS

The black one with the blue wing lyin' down at
the side.

MRS. PHELAN

Fine! Yes, ye've the color for the veil. And
ye'll not be buyin' it, Mrs. MacManus, for me
cousin'll lend it to ye— *(A gesture of protest
from Mrs. MacManus. Reassuring her)* And
glad of the chance, Mrs. MacManus. *(Mrs.
MacManus is sobbing regularly and with less
control each sob)* She's after showin' it to me.
It's that fine 'twould do y'r heart good. There,
now! And the hem, Mrs. MacManus, the hem!
*(Mrs. MacManus gives a rending sob, flings
up her two hands in agony nnd disappears.
The door shuts behind her. Mrs. Phelan shakes
her head after her in real sympathy)* The poor
young thing! *(Then she straightens up, taking
off her apron. Briskly)* I'll be steppin' out
now for the doctor. *(The smile leaves her face
and she nods her head reverently, talking as if*

in the presence of the corpse) And him that
was always so hearty. Poor young thing! Poor
young thing! *(She slips out, closing her door
quietly. All is still for a moment, then the faint
wind is again beginning to be heard. The door,
sixth floor left, opens and the crying of the
baby, distant from an inner room, comes down.
The Woman Sixth Floor Left rattles the dumb-
waiter rope and waits. There's a careful, faint
sound from the cellar, as the cellar door is
opened on a crack.)*

VOICE OF WOMAN SIXTH FLOOR LEFT
Mr. Kelly, there's no stame at all. *(Silence)*
There's not one drop of heat in the pipes and
the children comin' home from school. *(Silence,
with the breath of two people present in it)*
Y're there, Mr. Kelly, that I know. And I'll
have the landlord on ye, for y'r insubordina—
*(Door of fourth floor left opens. Joyous noise
of hungry children.)*

VOICE OF WOMAN FOURTH FLOOR LEFT
(a gentle, motherly voice) And here's the
children, Mr. Kelly, and the pipes—

VOICE OF LITTLE GIRL FOURTH FLOOR LEFT
Here's Johnny Phelan come for lunch, mither.

VOICE OF JOHNNY PHELAN
Me mudder's out.

VOICE OF WOMAN FOURTH FLOOR LEFT
(speaking into the room) Sit ye down there.

VOICE OF WOMAN SIXTH FLOOR LEFT
(loud) This is me last wurd, Mr. Kelly. The
breath is leavin' me body in the form of ice!

THE PROVINCETOWN PLAYS

*(There's a faint noise in the cellar of a door
cautiously closed.)*

VOICE OF WOMAN FOURTH FLOOR LEFT

(bright and ready for a talk) Ye're right, Mrs.
Tynan. He was there. *(The door above slams
shut. Speaking back into the room)* Be givin'
Johnny Phelan some of your tea. *(The door
closes. Again the sound of a faint wind. The
whistle, sixth floor left, blows, with flowery in-
direction; the cellar door opens and a man
whistles the first half of a phrase from Santa
Lucia. The door of the sixth floor left opens.)*

PLEASANT ITALIAN VOICE

Ice-a man, lady? *(A wail from the baby escapes.)*

VOICE OF WOMAN SIXTH FLOOR LEFT

(baited, angry) No! *(The Italian completes
with the phrase, closing the cellar door. Silence.
A moment of wind. The whistle, sixth floor
right, blows with irritable precision. The cellar door opens. Pause. Whistle: irritable
crescendo. Pause. Whistle. Pause.)*

VOICE OF GROCER

(Teutonic and disagreeable) De grozzer! Gott
in Himmel, dieses— *(Door closes with restrained fury. Silence. Sounds, left, from Mrs.
Phelan's kitchen. She is moving about. A siz-
zling and pleasant smell escapes, as her door
opens. She still has her hat on; her face is busy
and cheerful. She disappears a moment and
then reappears with part of bottle of milk and
part of a loaf of bread. She knocks quietly but
distinctly. She knocks a second time. The door*

194

right opens. Mrs. MacManus stands, weak and pale and patient.)

MRS. PHELAN

(handing the milk and bread across) Here's the mornin's milk, and y'r bread. *(Mrs. Mac-Manus takes them, putting them down right)* And here's— *(Mrs. Phelan turns back and brings up from the nearby table a tray with luncheon)* a bit of lunch I'm after fixin' for you. *(She hands it across)* Better late than never. Ye must eat, Mrs. MacManus, even with the black sorrow in the house.

MRS. MACMANUS

(in a weak voice) It's only a sup of tea I've had and the day near its end. The lump in me throat—but I'll try, Mrs. Phelan.

MRS. PHELAN

Be puttin' it on the table there, so's we can talk. *(Mrs. McManus does)* And himself— is he—

MRS. MACMANUS

(looking up, ready to take heart if she only may) He's a bit conscious now— *(Mrs. Phelan's face drops)* but I'm not darin' to hope.

MRS. PHELAN

Y're right, Mrs. MacManus. They're always better before they're worse. I left word with the doctor. *(Taking off her hat)* He was out deliverin' a woman. Awh, it's wonderful, Mrs. MacManus, the way a new soul comin' in brushes past the old one— *(pointing into Mrs. MacManus' room)* goin' out! *(Mrs. Mac-Manus chokes a bit on her toast. Cheering her)*

And now hear the good news. Me cousin's after lendin' ye the veil.

MRS. MACMANUS

(putting down her tea) Ah, the sharp sorrow's on me again at the word!

MRS. PHELAN

(mechanically undoing the package) Wisha, darlin', ye may never need it. And I have it right here. *(Mrs. MacManus pushes the tray aside. Ingratiating)* Will ye be seein' it? How soft it hangs! *(She is now holding the veil in the shaft)* And the hem—it's two inches, it is. Will ye be weighin' it, in y'r hand—it's that light.

MRS. MACMANUS

(weighing it) 'Tis light.

MRS. PHELAN

Where's the bit hat ye was tellin' me of?

MRS. MACMANUS

It's under the bed. Himself maybe will be seein' me.

MRS. PHELAN

And what if he does, darlin'? and the blue wing yet on it. *(Mrs. MacManus passes back the veil and disappears. Mrs. Phelan holds it up, half draping it. Mrs. MacManus hands over the hat.)*

MRS. MACMANUS

(a tremor in her voice) I've the scissors here.

MRS. PHELAN

Thanks. Be drinkin' y'r tea, that's the gurl. Easy on, *(She snips off the wing)* easy off. Let me see what way it looks on ye.

MRS. MACMANUS
(*putting it on deftly, giving a touch to her hair*)
It would be different with the wing off?
(There's a little worry in her voice.)

MRS. PHELAN
Ye should see the way it looks! And now be
tryin' the veil. I've the pins with me. *(She
passes one over.)*

MRS. MACMANUS
Ye're good to me, Mrs. Phelan, takin' all this
pains.

MRS. PHELAN
Oh, I'm enjoyin' it fine, Mrs. MacManus!
Now take the short end—that's it—and put it
— See if I can be reachin' you. Now pin that
back—there. Ah, now, will ye look! Ye were
born for the style! Ye should never wear anything else.

MRS. MACMANUS *(pleased)*
Ye like it fine? I'll have another pin if ye have
it.

MRS. PHELAN
The white neck of ye.

MRS. MACMANUS
It would look well?

MRS. PHELAN
And the hair of ye, lickin' out like a little flame
—and dancin' on y'r ear.

MRS. MACMANUS
(with desire) I wonder could I be seein' meself?

MRS. PHELAN
And what's to prevent?

MRS. MACMANUS *(smiling)*

Nothin' that I know. *(She turns toward the room)* I'll be gettin' the glass.

MRS. PHELAN

(in horror) Glory be to God, Mrs. MacManus, stop!

MRS. MACMANUS

(turning a face of pure disappointment) I could be goin' in on me toes. He's sleepin' fine.

MRS. PHELAN

Would ye kill the man, and this his last moment! Whst, wait. I'll be bringin' me own glass. *(She disappears. Mrs. MacManus fixes the folds, seeing them with her fingers. She hums a bit as she tries to see the effect of the long ripple of goods down her back. Mrs. Phelan reappears, holding out the glass)* Here, darlin'. Take the side look first. Ain't that pretty? And the white neck of ye gleamin' against the dark.

MRS. MACMANUS

(surveying it with pleasure) In his health he will be always kissin' it, will Pat.

MRS. PHELAN

And why not? and you lookin' like the queen of all Ireland—and the king dead. *(The door bell in the kitchen rings sharp. Mrs. MacManus, with a start, clutches her bosom.)*

MRS. MACMANUS

Mary, save me! What's that? *(They wait, listening.)*

MRS. PHELAN *(slowly)*

It's maybe the doctor. *(Mrs. MacManus turns*

abruptly, about to go in. Mrs. Phelan speaks in sharp alarm) Hould, woman! And you meetin' the doctor like that, he'll be havin' you up for murder.

MRS. MACMANUS

(going to pieces, in wild excitement and tearing the thing off her head) Ye'll all have the heart torn out of me, pullin' me this way and that. *(She thrusts over the hat and veil. The door-bell rings a second time. She disappears and the dumb-waiter door shuts.)*

MRS. PHELAN

(the hat on her hand and straightening out the folds) The Houly Mother protect them both; him dyin' and her breakin' her heart for the loss of him. *(Giving a last look at the hat and veil, exhibited on her hand)* The poor, pretty young thing! *(She closes the door, disappearing. The shaft grows dark and the wind keens a bit stronger. Door fourth floor left opens.)*

VOICE OF MAN FOURTH FLOOR LEFT

Well? No, Biddie, there's no one at the whistle. And I says to the boss— *(Door closes. Silence. Mrs. Phelan opens her door slowly, cautiously. She listens. Quiet. She gives a long, mournful sigh and closes the door. The baby on sixth floor left starts crying.)*

VOICE OF MAN SIXTH FLOOR LEFT

(near door) What the divil's the matter with him now?

VOICE OF WOMAN SIXTH FLOOR LEFT

Nothin's the matter, save his father's bad temp— *(Quiet. Mrs. Phelan opens her door,*

listens, shakes her head with sorrowful satis-
faction.)

MRS. PHELAN

Rest his soul. Whsst, Johnny! *(Johnny*
galumps near) Shh, a man's dyin' within. Be
goin' down to the door and see if the black
crêpe's up. *(Mrs. Phelan takes out a handker-*
chief and still listening keenly, begins to weep
and sniff.)

VOICE OF JOHNNY

(in a penetrating whisper) Not yet, mither!
I looked before.

MRS. PHELAN

(disappointed, but feelingly) It's a long pass-
in'. *(She closes door. Silence.)*

VOICE OF LITTLE GIRL

(fourth floor left) It's me *prayers* I'm doin',
mither. *(Pause.)*

VOICE OF MAN FOURTH FLOOR LEFT

Good-night, sweet Biddie Murphy. *(Silence.*
The wind keens a bit. Sleepy fretting of a
child. Slippered feet on oil-cloth, left. Mrs.
Phelan, her hair done smooth in a tight pig-
tail and in her night-gown, opens door. Listens.
Muffled comes the sound of a dog howling.)

MRS. PHELAN

(Crossing herself; on a voice that keens) God
rest his soul!

[THE CURTAIN DROPS AND IMMEDIATELY RISES,
TO INDICATE MORNING]

Baby sixth floor left wails and the father is heard
walking up and down and crooning to it. It

quiets. It is still. Silence. A dog gives two sharp barks. Silence. Faint but persistent comes the amorous antiphony of two cats. A pale, white light steals down the shaft. The steam is heard cracking and clanking in the cold pipes. The door sixth floor left opens, and a yellow light streams down. The man pulls up the empty dumb-waiter.

VOICE OF MAN SIXTH FLOOR LEFT

Damn that milkman! Why in hell can't he—
(Door slams shut. Immediately from the cellar comes a cheery young whistle, and the waiter flies down; four pairs of milk bottles are put on. The cellar door bangs shut.)

VOICE OF WOMAN SIXTH FLOOR LEFT

(sleep, sour) It's the milkman now, Mike.

VOICE OF MAN SIXTH FLOOR LEFT

I'm not goin' ter pull up that damned waiter again if— *(The door is shut. The baker's boy puts on the bread. He blows the eight whistles with vigor and delight. The door sixth floor right opens.)*

VOICE OF WOMAN SIXTH FLOOR RIGHT

(the easy, cheerful, young voice) It's the bread, Maggie. I'll be pullin' it up. *(Mrs. Phelan's door is seen opening on a crack. As the waiter passes the stage level, the hands of Johnny Phelan shoot out and he grabs off his mother's milk and bread. The waiter is yanked past and up and the pleasant voice grows angry)* I saw you, Johnny Phelan—you good-for-nothin' lazy lout. *(The hand and arm of Johnny Phelan project through the crack into the dumb-waiter*

shaft and the fingers of the hand temporarily attached to a nose wriggle in disdain) And if ever I get me two hands into your hair— *(Her door shuts. Johnny Phelan executes, unseen, a shuffle on the oilcloth.)*

MRS. PHELAN

(appearing suddenly) Ye black-hearted boy, dancin', and the man lyin' there in his coffin cold dead! *(Mrs. Phelan leans over and listens. In surprise)* There's no keenin'—not a sob. There's somethin' wrong! *(She knocks, calling)* Mrs.—Mac—Man—us. *(The door, right, opens suddenly and sharply and Mrs. MacManus is seen. She has on a house dress and apron and her sleeves are rolled up. Her eyes are bright, her cheeks flushed; her manner brisk, angry.)*

MRS. MACMANUS

Good-mornin', Mrs. Phelan—if ye can call it a good mornin' when y'r asked to go six ways at once and only one pair of feet for the goin'!

MRS. PHELAN

(with a fine regret in her voice) Then ye've saved him?

MRS. MACMANUS

Saved him! It's meself that needs savin' now. What with—"The newspaper, darlin' "—and —"A drink of water, me pretty"—and—"Is the coffee ready, mavourneen?" — and — it's meat he's yellin' for now!

MRS. PHELAN

Doctor Platz is the rare wonder.

MRS. MACMANUS

He's not. 'Twas nothin' but the two tonsils in his throat started all the roarin' and rampin' and preparin' us for his death. *(There's an empty pause.)*

MRS. PHELAN

(looking down the shaft; in a lying voice) Now —did I hear the ice man, Mrs. MacManus?

MRS. MACMANUS

(looking down and lying, too) I think maybe ye did. No, 'twas something else.

MRS. PHELAN

(beckoning her closer) I'll be takin' it back to me cousin, the morn.

MRS. MACMANUS

(regretfully, in pleasant reminiscence) It did become me, did it not, Mrs. Phelan?

MRS. PHELAN

That it did, Mrs. MacManus.

MRS. MACMANUS

(hesitating) Could I—be seein' it a minute?

MRS. PHELAN

(turning left and taking the hat and veil from the table near) I have it ready—sewed and the iron goin' over it.

MRS. MACMANUS

I wonder if— *(She listens back)* He's readin' the paper.

MRS. PHELAN

(handing over the hat and veil) I've the glass with me. *(Mrs. MacManus puts on the hat and veil, straightening the folds.)*

MRS. MACMANUS

It does hang nice and rich.

MRS. PHELAN

Ah, Mrs. MacManus, I'll never be happy till I see the like of it on y'r head again!

MRS. MACMANUS

(with a nervous glance over her shoulder) Be givin' me the glass! *(She takes it and smiles as she sees the reflection)* It does look grand. It sets me fine. Mrs. Phelan, I never put a thing on me head that pleased me more.

VOICE OF PAT

(from some distance; kind) Katy, darlin'!

MRS. MACMANUS

(in utter terror) It's himself!

VOICE OF PAT

(a little nearer; more insistent) Katy—

MRS. MACMANUS

(to him as she grabs off the hat and veil) Stand where ye are!—It's caught, Mrs. Phelan. *(Loud, back to Pat)* Out of the draft. *(After a moment fraught with agony, the veil is freed. She bundles it and the hat together and thrusts them over to Mrs. Phelan)* Tell y'r cousin—

VOICE OF PAT

(irritable) Kate—

MRS. MACMANUS

I'm comin' man!— The hat's hers and I'm thankin' her for the loan and sorry I can't be usin' it. *(Turning towards the room, with terrible irony)* Is it y'r five pounds of steak, Pat, y're wantin' now? *(The door shuts behind her.)*

MRS. PHELAN

Poor soul! *(Looking at the door angrily)* And him that hearty! *(She gives the veil a last sad look and fixing it as it hangs grand on her hand)* Ah, you never know the wurst till it comes. *(As she shuts the door in reproach and disappointment)* The poor, pretty young thing. *(As the curtain begins to descend two sharp whistles are heard.)*

VOICE OF JANITOR

Garbage!

[CURTAIN]

THE STRING OF THE SAMISEN

A PLAY

By Rita Wellman

Copyright, 1917,
By Rita Wellman

All Rights Reserved

THE STRING OF THE SAMISEN was originally produced by The Provincetown Players, New York, on January 17, 1919, with the following cast:

KATSU MORI, a rich merchant, *Ward Roege*
TAMA, his wife, *Edna St. Vincent Millay*
ARINORI OKUBO, *Rollo Peters*
SUTSUMI, teacher of the Samisen, *O. K. Liveright*
HATSU, Tama's maid, *Blanche Hays*

Setting by Lloyd Wright
Directed by Michio Itow

CHARACTERS

KATSU MORI, a rich merchant
TAMA, his wife
ARINORI OKUBO, a young samurai
SUTSUMI, teacher of the samisen
HATSU, Tama's maid
TWO YOUNG SAMURAI

The action takes place in Japan of the eighteenth century.

NOTE.—Although the theme of this play is taken from a Bushido legend, the author has used her material freely in her own way, but begs to be pardoned for any anachronisms.

THE STRING OF THE SAMISEN

SCENE: *Large room in the merchant's house. Three screens at back forming the walls. A space for an entrance between the foremost screens, the other placed in the background to form a passage. These screens are painted silver, with sprays of azaleas in faint pink. Shoji (paper windows) occupy the whole of the walls right and left. On the back screen left a kakémono. Beneath it a tall, white porcelain jar with a single iris flower. Mats on the floor right and left. A small lacquer table at left forward. It is afternoon. Hatsu, the maid, wearing a cotton crepe kimono, enters at back, and bows to the ground before Sutsumi, who comes in slowly, pointing his cane before him, as he is blind. He wears a grey crepe kimono and a scarf over his head; this he removes. He is old and grey.*

SUTSUMI
Hatsu-San, where is your mistress? Is she here?

HATSU
She is here, Sutsumi-San. I will call her. Your health is good, Sutsumi?

SUTSUMI
If the blind and old can be well. And you, Hatsu-San?

14

HATSU

I am young and strong and no evil spirit touches
me. *(Bows)* I will call my lady. *(She bows
again and goes out entrance at back. Tama
enters. She is a pretty, dainty creature, dressed
in an exquisite embroidered kimono of cherry-
colored silk. Her hair is arranged elaborately.)*

SUTSUMI *(bowing)*

O-Kami-San.

TAMA *(bowing)*

Sutsumi-San, how did you know that I had come
in?

SUTSUMI

I heard the rustle of your silk.

TAMA

And I am famous for my quiet walk! Be
seated. *(She sits on the mat left and he sits
on the mat right.)*

SUTSUMI

My lady is well?

TAMA

I am always well, thank you. And you?

SUTSUMI

I grow well when I hear my lady's voice.

TAMA

I am a very bad pupil. I have not practiced at
all. *(Claps her hands)* Hatsu must bring me
my samisen. After all, work is not pleasant.
The birds do not have to learn to sing. For my
part, I would rather play from morning until
night. There are many pleasant games to learn
if you are idle enough.

SUTSUMI
My lady is wise beyond her years.

HATSU
(*entering, bowing*) Here is your samisen, my lady. (*She hands Tama the samisen, a musical instrument something like a guitar, with three strings, and played with a small piece of ivory. Hatsu then goes out.*)

TAMA
Do you know any dances, Sutsumi?

SUTSUMI
Ladies of high degree do not dance!

TAMA
Oh, there you are wrong, Sutsumi. Everyone is dancing now. There is Haru-San. She knows a dance. It is as if she were being pursued by spiders. She is a very ugly woman and she has had ten children. Her husband has five concubines, and he is always threatening to divorce her because she is a gossip. But I think it is on account of her dancing.

SUTSUMI
It is not pleasant to think upon spiders.

TAMA
But I am sure there must be more alluring dances, if not necessarily designed for the entertainment of one's august husband.

SUTSUMI
All good things ladies learn are necessarily designed for the entertainment of their august husbands.

TAMA

    (with a sigh) I wonder how that started, Sutsumi?

SUTSUMI

    The law of human deportment sprang from the word of Buddha.

TAMA *(thoughtfully)*

    Yes, that is so. *(Quickly)* Sutsumi, I would like to learn a dance that is something like a song—a song with a body—a song that is the petal of a plum blossom in an April breeze.

SUTSUMI

    An imagination is a dangerous thing in a woman.

TAMA *(coaxingly)*

    Sutsumi, please play me a song. A swaying, dancing kind of song. I do not care where you learned it—if it comes from the secret houses of delight where men forget their honorable duties and which good women pass with their nostrils squeezed together—lest they breathe contamination.

SUTSUMI

    My lady!

TAMA

    Hurry! Play me a song. You go every place. You learn everything. Your eyes are blind, but the gods gave you eyes in your ears and fingers.

SUTSUMI

    I would play you such a song—but your lord—

TAMA

    Oh, you need not worry about him. My lord

is attending an important meeting of merchants.
My lord is never smiling these days. He has
traded honestly all his life, but he has somehow
made an enemy.

SUTSUMI

I cannot imagine how anyone should come to
hate your lord.

TAMA

Nor I. He is as harmless as a woman for all
his stormy looks. I do believe that the more
gentle he grows the darker he makes his face
purposely.

SUTSUMI

It is a disgrace to be soft in your ways when
you are a man. But is there no one to hear our
song?

TAMA

Only Hatsu. As you know, I live all alone.

SUTSUMI

You are favored of the gods.

TAMA

Yes, I am a fortunate woman. I have no
mother-in-law and my husband has no concubines. My house is my own. All my rich em-
broideries—my silk worms—even my garden.
My garden is my own, from the silver lake
with the lotus blossoms down to the smallest
snail.

SUTSUMI

Your life is free of shadows.

TAMA

I could not have more even if I were unre-
spectable. Yet the life of an oiran is an easy

one. To sing and dance all day long and to wear a gorgeous unabashed obi. To lure men from their honorable boredom. To smilingly make them forget their duties. Life in Japan is just duty after duty. How is that, Sutsumi?

SUTSUMI

I am teacher of the samisen, not the book of Wisdom. Play for me the song I gave you to learn and then we will learn a dance.

TAMA

(starts to play the samisen) When I sit by the garden wall and sing, I can hear footsteps grow slow on the other side. I should like to be a man and walk by a garden wall and hear a lady singing. *(She plays a moment falteringly, then puts down the samisen to talk)* Did you ever see an Englishman, Sutsumi? I know a lady who saw an Englishman. His nose started from his eyes like a demon, and his eyes were close together like a bird of prey. He did everything the wrong way, and he had no soul. What can you expect? In England the women rule; and there have been cases where a young girl of sixteen commands the life of five or even six young men.

SUTSUMI

England is a land of Barbarians.

TAMA

Children may be rude to their parents, and a wife may say no to her husband. The gods must be very fond of the English. *(Sings)*

Adana é- gao -ni
Mayowanu mono wa
Ki-Butsu- Kana- Butsu
Ishi -botoké.

SUTSUMI

Where did you learn that song, my lady? That is not one of my songs.

TAMA

(laughing gaily) I heard it on the street. A funny little boy was singing it. It is such an amusing little song. Does it shock you, Sutsumi?

SUTSUMI

If your lord should hear that song and believe that it was I who taught it to you—

TAMA

He will never hear it. *(Laughs gaily.)*

SUTSUMI

I cannot see why you laugh, my lady.

TAMA

The sunlight. You do not see the sunlight, Sutsumi. It is dancing on the floor—up from my pool in the garden. Oh, I am so happy to-day! I feel like a young tree. I am the child who has no punishment. You are so funny, Sutsumi, with your dark, still face. It is like the august house of the Kami with the never-opening doors.

SUTSUMI

When you have known all the sorrow I have known— The cherry blossom lasts for half a week, but sin and sorrow last all the year.

TAMA

I hate sad people. *(Sitting beside him)* Tell me something about life, then, since you know so much about it.

SUTSUMI

And do you know nothing about life, my lady?

TAMA

Only what nice women know. From the time I was a child until I was fifteen I had a few lessons——how to sew and how to sit and how to arrange flowers and pour tea and those fairy tales they tell us about the people in other lands. And, of course, always the talk of the old women about how children are born.

SUTSUMI

You were well educated.

TAMA

Then one day my father said to me, Tama, you are to have a husband. The day of splendor has come, I said to myself. Well, he came to see me. Our parents did all the talking. I saw him only out of the corner of my eyes. But I kept saying to myself: This my husband! This august monkey! This honorable grand-father! This mountain of cruelty!

SUTSUMI

I hope you obeyed your father's wishes?

TAMA

Oh, yes! I am the daughter of a samurai. I was brought up in obedience. It is life, I said. Life is not for love. Love is for the gods and geishas. We were married. I received more bright silks for my dowry than any maiden in my town, and the gifts that passed back and forth were worthy of royalty.

SUTSUMI

You were happy?

TAMA

No. Bright silks and a dowry of nice things do not make a happy marriage. My mother-in-law showed me the way of hell. I soon went home to my father's house. That is all I know about life, Sutsumi.

SUTSUMI

Your second lord is kind and rich. You are happy now?

TAMA

Yes, he is kind. He never scolds me, and he never reproaches me for having no children. But who knows, that may not be entirely my fault.

SUTSUMI

My lady!

TAMA

Your being blind makes me believe you deaf also. *(Suddenly catching up the samisen)* Let us sing a song that is gay—gay as a blue sky in a clear pool where there are lotus flowers, and swans with proud necks, and the mysterious faces of two lovers who are vowed to each other for seven lives.

SUTSUMI

I know no such song.

TAMA

Then invent one.

SUTSUMI

My heart has no clear pools—only valleys of snow.

TAMA

Then I will. *(Plays and recites)*

How dark is the pool.
But now a soft light shines there—
Two lovers are drinking—
They do not see their shadows
Among the watery flowers.

SUTSUMI

That is not gay, my lady. Shadows mean death.

TAMA

Some spirit compelled me. I will sing a gay song now. *(She starts to play, but as she does so the string of her samisen snaps.)*

SUTSUMI *(startled)*

What was that?

TAMA

The string of my samisen snapped.

SUTSUMI *(mysteriously)*

Do you know what that means?

TAMA

It means something, Sutsumi?

SUTSUMI

The dancing girls have a superstition, that when the string of the samisen snaps lovers will be parted.

TAMA *(rising)*

Lovers will be parted!

SUTSUMI

Lovers; not husband and wife!

TAMA *(alarmed)*
Yes—lovers. Sutsumi, my lesson is ended for to-day. You may leave me now.

SUTSUMI
Surely an honorable wife can have nothing to fear from the snapping of the samisen string.

TAMA
To fear? I do not fear. Please go now, Sutsumi.

SUTSUMI
My lady, your voice is like the trembling of leaves.

TAMA
An evil spirit possessed my song—that is all.

SUTSUMI
Let me take your samisen. I will put in a new string.

TAMA
(clinging to it) No! No! I will keep my samisen!

SUTSUMI
(preparing to go) As my lady wishes. *(Feeling about with his stick)* That is the way to my lady's apartments. There is the shoji. There is the entrance to my lady's house. Am I right?

TAMA
(handing something he has dropped) Yes, you are right, Sutsumi. *(Leading him back)* It is fortunate to be old and blind. Then one sees only the light. One is not groping in the dark ways of love.

SUTSUMI

The honorable lady and the dancing girl are both flowers—but they bloom in different seasons. *(Bowing very low)* My lady—my lady has nothing to fear.

TAMA

Good-bye, Sutsumi.

SUTSUMI

(bowing low at the door) Good-bye, my lady. *(Sutsumi goes out. Tama sits and takes her samisen and places a new string in it. Hatsu enters presently in great excitement.)*

HATSU

My lady!

TAMA *(impatiently)*

Don't breathe so loud. What is wrong with you?

HATSU

The teacher of the samisen!

TAMA

(after a moment) Coming now?

HATSU

Here, my lady! He has taken off his disguise at the outer door.

TAMA

(in excitement) Hurry! Bring me my toilet case. I look like an old hag. Where is my new kimono? Oh, Hatsu, why did you make me wear this ugly thing to-day? Hurry! *(She rushes to back and gets a heavy silk kimono of rich embroidery, which she puts on over the other. Hatsu brings the toilet case and Tama*

220

sits before it and powders her face and darkens her lips.)

HATSU

Here he is, my lady! *(Tama rises in great confusion, but controls herself and waits with dignity and calm. Arinori Okubo enters.)*

ARINORI *(bowing)*

My lady!

TAMA *(bowing)*

My lord! *(To Hatsu, who lingers)* Hatsu! *(Hatsu runs out, taking the toilet case with her.)*

ARINORI

It is I!

TAMA

Arinori!

ARINORI

You did not expect me, then?

TAMA

No. I thought it was only my old blind teacher.

ARINORI *(ardently)*

My beautiful one!

TAMA

Do not come too close. Your face is like the moon, Arinori—rising after a night of pain. Stay there. I cannot breathe when my life is coming back to me so fast. The gods when they visit the earth must know how sweet it is to breathe after so long a breathlessness.

ARINORI

My hands have thirsted for your touch. *(He takes her hands.)*

TAMA

Oh, sacred sin of loving! I am ready to join a thousand restless demons and go wailing about the earth forever for the sake of this moment.

ARINORI

Your lips are like the saké wine they prepare for children at The Feast of Dolls.

ARINORI

My love!

TAMA

My lord! *(They embrace.)*

ARINORI

Tama, my child, you must listen to me. Sit here. I must tell you something of importance. Where is your maid?

TAMA *(loudly)*

At the screen listening. *(Laughing as Hatsu is heard running away)* Wherever Hatsu goes there are holes in the shoji. My love, your face to-day is as fierce and brilliant as the sun himself. What is the matter?

ARINORI

Tama, there is one in the city who is plotting against me and my kind—the noble samurai. He has raised ant hills of spies against us. Our privileges are being encroached upon—our immortal rights. Our very lives are in danger from this man, such an evil power he has. And to meet him no one would know—not even those who live in the same house with him would suspect—that he is possessed of a thousand devils.

222

TAMA

Arinori, the man must be a demon to plot against you. But why do you come here to talk of such rough things? You have not even told me that I look beautiful.

ARINORI

You do look beautiful. You always look beautiful.

TAMA

I do not like to be told that I always look beautiful. I like to be told that I look beautiful *now*.

ARINORI

Tama, you are the daughter of a samurai. You must give me your help.

TAMA

Oh, do not ask me to do anything wicked, Arinori. I cannot do anything evil. I am just your little almond flower. Why should I risk my frailness in men's rough affairs?

ARINORI

Do you not want to help me, Tama?

TAMA *(seductively)*

I will help you. In your tea house by the river. The priests talk about paradise in eternity, but we know better, Arinori. Hurry there now; I will meet you.

ARINORI

This is serious, Tama.

TAMA

Is there anything more serious than love?

ARINORI

There is death.

TAMA

Death is not serious at all when it is for love's sake.

ARINORI

There is one thing more serious than love and death.

TAMA

What is that?

ARINORI

There is duty.

TAMA

Duty! Do not talk to me of duty. To hear people talk in Japan you would imagine there was nothing in life but duty.

ARINORI

Tama, the man who is plotting against me is Katsu Mōri.

TAMA

My husband!

ARINORI

Now you understand.

TAMA

My husband! You are his enemy then? You, Arinori Okubo?

ARINORI

He is *my* enemy.

TAMA

You two are enemies?

ARINORI

He must die.

TAMA

Oh, no, Arinori!

ARINORI

He is starting a rebellion—he wants to kill the samurai. He is a dangerous man. If his kind is allowed to live they will crush out the flower of Japan, her beautiful tradition of nobility and chivalry.

TAMA

He only wants to sell his silks, Arinori. I know that. He has told me so hundreds of times. He wants to be allowed to trade in peace, that is all. Hasn't he a right to trade?

ARINORI

It is vulgar to trade. He must die. My honored father is dead. I have no brothers. I alone represent the dignity of my house. In the honor of my noble name I must kill this man.

TAMA

But my husband, Arinori!

ARINORI

And you must help me.

TAMA

No, no! That I cannot do. Not even for your sake, Arinori. Not even for you.

ARINORI

(going back) You do not love me then.

TAMA

(following him) Arinori, what are you saying? I do not love you! Come, we will think of another way. I will think of something. Do not run away from me. Do not leave me like that. *(She goes on her knees before him)* Do not be cruel to me, Arinori.

ARINORI
(turning, threateningly) You will do as I wish?

TAMA
Oh, my dear, my dear—

ARINORI
Answer me, Tama.

TAMA
I have been wicked. I have been drowning in sweet wine.

ARINORI
You regret my love.

TAMA
I cannot sin twice. Ask me anything, Arinori—anything but that.

ARINORI
I demand that you help me, Tama.

TAMA
(in an awed voice) Arinori, do you know that the bond between husband and wife is sacred and endures for two lives?

ARINORI
Will you help me?

TAMA
Your voice is like thunder. It is shaking my roots.

ARINORI
You will?

TAMA
Think of what you ask me, my beloved.

ARINORI
(going back) Everything is ended from now on.

TAMA

(calling) Arinori! Arinori!

ARINORI

You consent?

TAMA

(after a pause—bowing her head very low)
Yes.

ARINORI

(coming near her) Listen to me, Tama. You
must see that he returns home to-night.

TAMA

Yes.

ARINORI

He has stayed out the whole night recently?

TAMA

Yes.

ARINORI

When he does come home he is usually late,
is he not?

TAMA

Yes.

ARINORI

He must sleep in the room which opens to the
gallery—the room which faces the garden.

TAMA

Yes—our sleeping room.

ARINORI

Your sleeping room, yes. You must have a
lantern. When he is asleep you must pass it
back and forth slowly—three times—before
the shoji of his room. Do you understand?

TAMA

Three times—slowly.

ARINORI
   It will be the signal.

TAMA
   The signal.

ARINORI
   We will come from the street. We will make
   our escape through the garden. The amada
   must be ready for us to pass in. My sword is
   the carved sword of my ancestors. It will kill
   him augustly and with honor.

TAMA
   Yes.

ARINORI
   Do you understand all?

TAMA
   Yes, my lord—all.

ARINORI
   Rise and look into my face, Tama. *(She rises
   and goes to him)* Do you love your husband?

TAMA
   I love you, Arinori. When you came you were
   the answer to all prayers. You were the vision
   of all dreams. I have envied none—not even
   the gods.

ARINORI
   Your servants must see nothing. They must
   be away.

TAMA
   Everything shall be done as you say.

ARINORI
   Three times—slowly. Do you remember?

TAMA
   I remember.

ARINORI
(putting on the cloak of the samisen teacher)
When he is gone there will be no more separations.

TAMA
Arinori, I do not know you now. Your eyes are as terrible as a blue-flaming sword.

ARINORI
A merchant to insult a samurai! My august father ripped open his own bowels with his knife rather than allow an inferior to conquer him. My sister flung herself into the sea to drown rather than yield to her father's enemy —and she loved him. I wear the armor of my ancestors in my heart.

TAMA
I bow before your terribleness, my lord. Your will shall be obeyed.

ARINORI
Your lover will be yours forever, Tama—after to-night.

TAMA
After to-night.

ARINORI
Remember all that I have told you—and be cautious.

TAMA
I will be cautious. *(He goes out with much dignity. Tama stands awed and frightened. Then she calls faintly—Hatsu!)*

HATSU
(entering) Yes, my lady! What is the matter, my lady?

TAMA

Nothing—nothing is the matter. Only that I am a woman. The silver crown of sorrow that all women must wear is coming down upon my white forehead. I am a daughter blessed by the gods. I am a child with no punishments. But the gods are men and the world is the dwelling place of men. We are only the pleasure flowers who suffer eternally that we may be fragrant for a single day.

HATSU

I never saw my lady sad.

TAMA

No. I was playing a game. I was a may-fly who pretends that one summer day will last forever. But how quickly the cold night comes. *(She shudders.)*

HATSU

My lady! *(She begins to whimper and wipe her eyes with her sleeve.)*

TAMA

(stamping her foot) Hatsu! I am a daughter of a samurai. I despise your wet sleeve. Go and leave me alone.

HATSU

Yes, my lady. *(She goes out. Tama, after a moment, picks up her samisen listlessly and examines the new string. She then sits down and plays, singing in a strained voice which attempts to be gay.)*

Adana é—gao ni
May o wanu mono wa

Ki-Butsu—Kana-Butsu
Ishi—botoké.

END OF SCENE

The curtain goes up almost at once. It is the same room arranged as a sleeping room. Hatsu is unrolling the beds for the night. The small lacquer table is placed at right. On the right wall, well forward, a large red lacquer chest. Lighted lanterns, one right and one left, well down. A faint light comes through the shoji at right from a lantern outside. Tama enters.

TAMA
My lord has come at last.

HATSU
Yes, my lady. Everything is ready. I will bring the tea.

TAMA
Yes, bring the tea, Hatsu. (*Katsu Mori enters. He is a large man, past middle age.*)

TAMA (*bowing*)
My lord!

KATSU
Tama! Still awake? It is very late.

TAMA
I waited for you, my lord.

KATSU
(*seating himself with satisfaction on the mat furthest left*) How quiet is my own home after the harsh voices of men. Why do we strive for riches in this world, Tama, when the mats are ready laid at home? (*Hatsu enters, bring-*

231

ing a small lacquer tray with tea. She places this on the table before Tama. She then goes to close the amada (the wooden outside shutters.)

TAMA

(as Hatsu puts down the tea) Thank you, Hatsu. *(as Hatsu is about to close the shutters)* Do not close the amada, Hatsu; I must have air to-night.

HATSU

I thought your lord—

KATSU

The amada must be closed; it may rain. It is almost morning.

TAMA

I have a headache. I cannot breathe when the amada is tight shut. May she not leave the amada open a little on that side, my lord?

KATSU

I was thinking only of your health, Tama. Leave the amada open, Hatsu.

HATSU

Yes, master. *(To Tama)* Everything is attended to, my lady. Good-night, my master and mistress. *(She goes out.)*

TAMA

Will you have tea now, Katsu?

KATSU

Thank you, Tama. *(He lights a pipe which stands on a low table at his bedside)* The life of a woman is an easy one. Singing songs and being beautiful and living only for love. It is only men who know how evil the world is.

TAMA

We live only to please, Katsu.

KATSU

My friends tell me that I have a self-willed wife, who reads too many romantic books. But you are always gentle and obedient, Tama.

TAMA

I hope I have pleased you, my lord.

KATSU

Your first husband spoiled you. That is why you ran away from him. But I do not spoil you. I demand obedience and modesty in a woman. You do not have children, it is true; but who knows, there may be some spell upon you.

TAMA

Katsu—

KATSU

All tell me that I should have concubines in my house that I might have a son and heir. But I cannot do it. When the lotus flower blooms in the pool you do not plant weeds.

TAMA

Thank you, Katsu. *(She rises and takes him a cup of tea, which she accidentally drops, breaking the thin cup to pieces)* Oh, Katsu, what have I done? May the gods punish me for being so clumsy! I have never dropped a tea cup before in my life. Katsu, forgive me.

KATSU

Your hand is trembling. What is the matter?

TAMA

I have something to tell you.

KATSU *(stretching)*

    I am too ready for sleep. It is late. It will not be long before the bell rings in the temple.

TAMA

    I must tell you, Katsu. Two things happened: I sang a song and shadows came into it, when I willed only the sun. And—the string of my samisen snapped.

KATSU

    What do you know of such things? That is the talk of dancing girls.

TAMA

    Sutsumi told me. It means lovers parting. Katsu, we must part to-night—at once. Your life is in danger.

KATSU

    Tama, what is this? *(Jumps to his feet.)*

TAMA

    There is a plot against you. I heard it to-day. They are coming here—here to this room— they are just waiting for you to sleep so that they can kill you.

KATSU

    My enemies are planning this to-night? Tama, how could you hear this?

TAMA

    Don't ask me. You must run away. You must go at once—every minute is precious. We haven't a minute now. I have planned everything.

KATSU

    I do not know what to believe. How can you

plan for me? What am I to do? I do not
understand all this.

TAMA

Go; do not stand and talk. Katsu, hurry—
hurry for your life. Go out along the path
under the arbor to the pool. By the gate Sutsumi waits for you—he knows everything—he
knows the way—he can find his way in the dark.
Trust yourself into his hands.

KATSU

How can I let a woman make plans for me—
and trust myself into a blind man's hands? I
will not go; I will stay and defend myself.

TAMA

Do not be too proud to let me help you, Katsu.
Do as I ask. Even if you stay—there are other
nights. They will find a way to get in. You
cannot always be on guard. Katsu, go! Every
minute you stay makes it so hard for me.

KATSU

Why for you?

TAMA

Because I am concerned for your sake. Go—
go for the honor of your name.

KATSU

How do I know if this is true? It may be some
lie that has been told to frighten me and make
me ridiculous. How can you, a woman, hear
of such plots?

TAMA

I know—I know it all. I even know your enemy's name.

235

KATSU

You know my enemy's name!

TAMA

It is Arinori Okubo.

KATSU

You do know. He has planned to kill me, then. I will stay and fight him.

TAMA

Katsu, go—I beg of you to go. For the honor of our house, for the honor of your name. You cannot fight him; he is a samurai and skilled in the art of the sword. If you are killed there will be another war between the merchants and the samurai.

KATSU

And if I go—

TAMA

You see—you know I speak the truth. It is right. That is why my samisen string snapped to-day.

KATSU

But you, Tama!

TAMA

They will not harm a woman.

KATSU

Then— *(Turns toward the shoji left.)*

TAMA *(anxiously)*

Then—

KATSU

I will go—for the sake of peace and the honor of my house. *(He opens the amada, left, and stands ready to go.)*

236

TAMA

(going to him) Along the path under the arbor. Sutsumi waits for you by the gate. Do everything Sutsumi says. *(Kneeling)* My lord, if I have not always been obedient and gentle, I beg of you to forgive me. I have been self-willed—I have been ambitious and read too much from books about matters which are only for my superiors—my lord and his friends. In my blood is the proud strain of the samurai. I have not bowed to my lord as I should have done.

KATSU

(putting his hand on her head) I forgive you all, Tama. I go unwillingly because you wish it. Protect the honor of my house like a brave daughter of the samurai. (He goes out. During the following the light of dawn gradually comes through the shoji. Tama goes to the table, right, and writes a letter. She then goes to the chest, right, and gets a white silk kimono, which she puts on over the other kimono. She gets a thick, red belt from the chest, which she takes with her to the bed nearest the left shoji. With this belt she fastens her legs tightly together. She has laid the letter before her at the foot of the bed. She lies down on the mat and pulls a thick, silk quilt over her so that only the top of her head is visible. Hatsu enters. She carries a lantern. She goes, right, and pulls back the amada the entire distance it will go.)*

TAMA

Hatsu!

HATSU *(tremulously)*

Oh, my lady!

TAMA

Are you ready?

HATSU

I am so afraid!

TAMA

Quick! *(Hatsu goes falteringly to the shoji, right, and waves the lantern across it three times slowly. She opens the shoji and three men come in. Arinori rushes to the bed and stabs into the quilt with his sword. Hatsu utters a cry of horror.)*

ARINORI

(coming forward) Katsu Mori is no longer my enemy. *(As he sheathes his sword he sees Tama's letter and picks it up)* Reads—

As the shadow to the tree,

As the kernal to the fruit,

So am I to thee.

But the wife heart cannot beat in disobedience;

The red blood of Tama

Will wash away the quarrel of lord and lover.

TAMA *(moaning)*

Arinori!

ARINORI

(rushing to her) Tama! What is this? What have I done? Oh, the gods have hated me! My darling! *(He pulls back the quilt and sees her wounded)* Tama! *(He lifts her in his arms)* My flower! My beautiful moon!

NOT SMART

A FARCE IN ONE ACT

By Wilbur Daniel Steele

CHARACTERS

MILO TATE
FANNIE TATE, his Wife
MRS. PAINTER
MATTIE, the Maid
MR. SNOW, Fisherman

TIME—*Late this Summer*
PLACE—*A Cape Cod Village*

NOT SMART

SCENE—*The living room of a typical shore cottage—the rented kind; outer door, rear center; door to kitchen, left; writing desk against wall, right; two or three chairs, cheap stand, etc.*

Curtain discovers Milo stretched on the couch reading a magazine, and Fannie writing at the desk. Milo closes the magazine slowly, holds it away from him over the edge of the couch and, with an expression of exhausted hopelessness, lets it fall to the floor. He groans feebly.

MILO

What's the use? What's the use?

FANNIE

(turning a face, sympathetic but preoccupied)
Something in the magazine, dear?

MILO

(letting his feet hang over, speaks in a wearied, sing-song voice) The strange woman's face in the throng—pale, alluring, baffling—with lips like the poppy—and that sort of thing. The wind carving her figure as in warm and sentient marble. Ankles and so on. Perfectly inflamed, our hero pursues her, careless of the hereafter, reckless of the eyes of the world. Of a sudden, a vision of his beloved one—at home, you know—right in the middle of the street—flam-

243

ing sword sort of thing—and—and—I didn't read any further. I don't need to. I know he'll turn around and go home, Fannie. *Home!*

FANNIE

(still busy with her letter) Fancy!

MILO

(starting up with a feverish energy and kicking the magazine across the floor) They're all the same. That's what's the matter with America! *(Relapses on the couch, crosses his arms over his head and goes on speaking to the ceiling in a tone of musing)* Thank God—er—that is— the *gods*—nothing like that can ever happen to us. Isn't it fearful to think of one's spirit cooped up between four narrow walls like that? *(Fannie nods, without turning her head)* Now *I* would have followed that ankle, wouldn't I? I would have followed it till it—till it turned to ashes in my—huh-hum—well, you know. And then, when I came back to you enriched, bringing the spoils of a profound experience, Fannie—you wouldn't mind!

FANNIE

(looking up now) Mind? Why should I mind, Milo? Can a thing of that *sort* tamper with the essential qualities of our relationship? No, No! We've learned better than that, you and I.

MILO

(sitting up again, with waxing enthusiasm) And you! You'll always feel quite free, too? You'll never let the silly little inhibitions—

FANNIE *(energetically)*

No, no!

MILO

Some day there may be a nice chap—I'd rather have it a nice chap—

FANNIE

Like Mort, say.

MILO

(with a slight start) Mort *Painter?* *(Fannie's attention has returned to her letter once more. She folds it, puts it in an envelope and addresses it. Milo, studying her with a light of uneasy speculation, goes on after a moment)* I'm afraid it would raise a bit of the devil in the Painter house, Fannie; that's all. You know, Mrs. Painter isn't exactly—our kind. *(Fannie, still about her business, rises and places the letter among others on top of the desk. After another moment, Milo breaks out in a tone of obvious relief)* But he isn't home, you know.

FANNIE

(turning suddenly to face him) And *why* isn't he home? *Why* is he staying away so long? It's over *two months* now that he's been away.

MILO

(at a loss) Why—why—I don't know. He probably finds the fishing good down there in Maine, or wherever he is. I—I hadn't thought.

FANNIE

I had. Milo, there's something in the woodpile, I tell you. Mrs. Painter is distinctly evasive. It's all so unnatural. We all came down to this corner of the shore to have a nice, quiet summer. And then, of a sudden, *he packs up* and is gone over night—and no sign of his coming back. There's *something* behind it, Milo.

MILO

(rising and pacing the floor — petulantly) Pshaw-pshaw! There's the woman cropping out. Pshaw! Why shouldn't he go off fishing and stay as long as he wants to?

FANNIE

(ignoring the outburst) I've been thinking of nothing for a week but Mort.

MILO

(stopping short and staring at her) You *have!* *(After an instant of confrontation, he sits down weakly on the couch, mops his brow with his handkerchief, and then recovers himself sufficiently to resume in a tone tinctured with venom)* I must say, Fannie, this rather sudden interest in one of my oldest friends—

FANNIE

You don't *mind?*

MILO

Mind? *(He has the grace to blush)* Oh, m-m-mind? Why, good heavens, Fannie, wh-wh-why should I *mind?*

FANNIE

I *knew* you wouldn't. And, after all, it's his *wife* I'm concerned about. Poor thing— stranded here all alone.

MILO

(more than ever ashamed of himself, mopping his brow vigorously) Whew! It's darned hot, I say! I think I'll have a glass of milk, if you'd be so good, Fannie. That's a dear. *(As Fan-*

246

*nie crosses to door at left and calls out) Mattie!
Mattie! (Voice off-stage)* Huh?

FANNIE

Bring Mr. Tate a glass of milk—right away.
And how many times have I told you to say
"ma'am" when you speak to me?

MILO *(deprecatingly)*

Why *should* she say ma'am? After all, my
dear, you know she is—

FANNIE

(turning upon him with some petulance) There
are times, Milo, when your theories—

MILO *(quickly)*

My theories, Frances, are *identical* with yours;
the only point of variance being that *I* am willing to practice them *at home. (Rising, he trans-
fixes his wife with a didactic forefinger)* We
all talk so largely of the Brotherhood of Man.
And yet here is a young girl, a really splendid
sort of a creature in a way, living close to the
throbbing heart of Mother Earth.

FRANCES *(interrupting)*

Close to the throbbing heart of the kitchen
range, you'd better say. For all your fine talk,
you don't know any more about her than I do,
and that's not a blessed thing—not one single
blessed thing, Milo. For all we know, she may
be—oh, for heaven's sake, Milo, stop looking
that way!

MILO

(resuming with a heavy, ironical patience)
Living close to the throbbing heart of Mother
Earth, feeling the life-pulse of the Cosmos—

well—damn it all—she's precisely the kind of thing we write about and talk and make gestures about, the lot of us—*you* know. Only she *is* it. She *lives* it. She's got something we've lost. Sometimes, you know, my dear, I almost feel—I *do* feel—in a way—

FANNIE *(coolly)*
Yes?

MILO
A strange spiritual bond with that creature—something drawing me—irresistibly—like the pull of green things and the damp earth—weird—almost—ah—*Pliocene*—ugh—by the way, you don't mind?

FANNIE *(with difficulty)*
Mind?

MILO
(chin in hand). In a way, you know, she's got something or other that we— *(Enter Mattie, carrying a glass of milk on a server.)*

MILO
Ah! *(With an unwonted energy he moves a small stand beside the couch, half reclines, and waves Mattie to deposit the glass on the stand. As she does so he gently captures her hand in his. She endeavors to recover it, profoundly embarrassed, casts a frightened glance at the mistress, then, evidently deciding in her numb and docile brain that this is the accepted thing, remains inert, staring ponderously at her boot-toes. Milo resumes in a tone of dreaming)* I wonder if you've ever thought much about yourself, Mattie? You wouldn't, though. You

wouldn't—that's just the matter with *us*. No, of course you *wouldn't*—*(Turning to Fannie)* She wouldn't, would she? *(Turning back)* We've been wondering if you knew how wonderful you are, Mattie? Because you *are* wonderful. You're out of your age. In a world staggering under a Freud, a Trotsky, a Marconi, the Republic of China, and the Imagist Poets—you've managed somehow to slip back to the great, all-brooding fundamentals—Food—Shelter—Procreation—

FANNIE

Milo!

MILO

(impatiently, to Fannie) That, I believe, is the order in which they come. *(Lights cigarette)* Or—perhaps I'm wrong. Of course, my dear, if you want to get into philosophics and metaphysics—I grant you the old argument—does the hen come first and the egg second, or the egg first and the hen—

FANNIE

Milo! That is a *young girl!* *(Exit Mattie.)*

MILO

(with an air of hopelessness, shaking his head slowly) Frances, Frances, are we to be always like that? Always slipping back into the old fog-bound superstitions of the mid-Victorian home?

FANNIE

Oh, be quiet, please. It isn't that! You ought to know me well enough by this time. But—but she wouldn't understand. If she could understand—if it would do her any good—enlarge her life—*in the least,* Milo—

MILO

Understand? Of course she doesn't understand. Do we want her to understand, my dear girl? Enlarge her life? Look, here, my dear, I'm serious. That girl *has* got something or other that neither you nor I—or any of us in the—the group—could come to in a thousand years of self-centered and spiritual crucifixion— She has got—

FANNIE *(ironically)*

Exactly *what?* *(Rising.)*

MILO

(inexpressibly shocked at the Philistine question) Why, *Fannie!* Why—why, she has got —she's got—see here, Frances, you know what I mean as well as I do. For heaven's sake, after two years of our talks—our trying to find the—the—in our little group, you know— Look here, Fannie, you've talked as primitive as anyone. And now you stand there and ask— *(Glancing out of the window, he speaks with an air of relief at the diversion)* Oh, here comes Mrs. Painter up the steps.

FANNIE

(in confusion, extending the half-smoked cigarette) Oh, quick! Take this! *(Milo starts to take it, furtively; then, as if bethinking himself, draws back and confronts her with a grim disapprobation.)*

MILO

Fannie!

FANNIE

You *idiot!* (*A knock is heard at the door. Fannie, wasting no time in further argument, skips about in desperate search for a place to hide the incriminating object.*)

MILO

(*even more sternly*) *Frances!* Are we to be always *that—that—kind?* (*Fannie faces him defiantly; then, shamed by his superior sense of honor, puts the cigarette between her lips and puffs conscientiously. Knocking resumes*) Come in! (*Enter Mrs. Painter.*)

MRS. PAINTER

(*with a moderate effusiveness—to Milo*) Oh, good afternoon, Mr. Tate. I was just coming up from the beach, you know, and I thought I'd— (*Catching sight of Fannie in a cloud of smoke, she gasps, stares desperately at the floor, the ceiling, the desk; then sinks down in a chair*) —drop in!

MILO (*suavely*)

Terribly glad. When's Mort coming home?

MRS. PAINTER (*ill at ease*)

I—I—he hasn't decided. (*In haste to change the subject*) Hasn't it been a glorious— (*Suffers another shock as her eyes, turning, come to the pillar of smoke, and relapses.*)

FANNIE

(*hastily coughing as she inhales by accident*) Per-perfectly *glorious*, really. Yes, yes— When's Mort coming home?

MRS. PAINTER

I—I—he hasn't— (*Looks from one to the*

251

other with a sudden suspicion; then rises majestically and confronts Fannie with an icy accusation) Mrs. Tate, your husband asked me that question ten seconds ago, and, if I am not mistaken, you heard me answer him. *(Bursting into tears and stamping her feet)* Oh, oh, oh! I won't stand it! Oh, you're so *mean*—always pecking at me—

MILO *(aghast)*
Pecking?

FANNIE *(the same)*
Pecking at you?

MRS. PAINTER
Yes, *pecking* at me! *(She sinks down in the chair, and, burying her face in her hands, gives way to uncontrollable grief. The others exchange inquiring glances, shrug their shoulders, and sign with the helpless bewilderment of the falsely accused. By and by Mrs. Painter begins to speak, her cheeks pressed in her palms, eyes fixed on vacancy)* I suppose you might as well know. You'll have to, some time. Mort—is —never—coming—back!

FANNIE
W h a t !

MILO
Old Mort? Good old Mort? For heaven's sake, *why* not?

MRS. PAINTER
You remember the maid we engaged down here the first of the summer—Abbie Small? Well, she got in trouble. Oh yes, Mort denied it— and denied it and denied it. He would, of

course. We got her out of the way immediately; sent her up to the Rescued Magdalene's Home in the city. We couldn't do less. I know the place; it's good and clean and wholesome—not at all like an institution. They have their amusements and things. And—and— *(She suffers a momentary relapse into tears. Milo begins to pace the floor, wrapped in thought. She resumes gravely)* And Mort, when he found at last that the wool *would not* be pulled over my eyes, packed up his things and went away. . . . Perhaps it is best.

MILO

(wheeling on her) Best! You can say—*Best?* My God! *(Noting her look of alarm, in a gentler tone)* You must forgive me, Mrs. Painter. *(Sitting down on the end of the couch, he goes on with the persuasive sweetness of the evangelist)* You say it is best, by your lights. And by *my* lights, I say it is *worse*. Worse, because it seems to me you are missing the fundamental significance of life; that you are deliberately shutting the door on life; that you are throwing away an—experience! You three! Think of it! How wonderful a thing! Passing together, hand in hand, through the unfolding hours of a miracle! You three!

MRS. PAINTER

(recovering the faculty of speech at last) Are you *crazy?* *(Appealing to Fannie)* Is—is the man—*insane?*

FANNIE

(with a smile, half sad, half lifted) No, Mrs.

253

Painter. It seems to me he is precisely—*sane*.
We have been thinking about it a good deal—
Milo and I, and we—

MRS. PAINTER *(rising)*

Mrs. Tate! I can't say how *deeply* I am—I—
Really, I think I'd better be going. *(She moves
away majestically toward the door.)*

FANNIE

(intercepting her) Now-now! Don't take on
so, my dear. Pshaw! You musn't go off in a
huff like this—must she, Milo? See here; sit
down and we'll have a cup of tea. . . . *(Calling)* Mattie! Mattie!

MILO

Yes, yes—do please sit down. *(Calling)* Mattie! Mattie! *(Aside)* Where is that girl? *(To
others)* Wait a second; I'll go hurry her up.
(Exit.)

MRS. PAINTER

(sobbing gently into her handkerchief) But
my dear, my dear. You couldn't talk that way
—either of you—if you had been through it
yourselves—if you know—if you knew the tor-
ment of that day—when the girl came to me
and told me she wasn't smart.

FANNIE *(quizically)*

Not smart?

MRS. PAINTER

Yes. That's the way they put it down here—
when they are—*expecting*.

FANNIE

How quaint! Not smart. Fancy. *(Enter*

Milo) Oh, Milo, my dear, Mrs. Painter has just been telling me the quaintest thing.

MRS. PAINTER

(drawing up and recovering her dignity) It is a thing I should rather not discuss in—in—*mixed* company. Especially with *Mr. Tate.*

MILO

Oh, come now, Mrs. Painter. Don't let's quarrel over—over—abstractions. See here, we'll have some tea and we'll all feel better. . . . Where's that girl? *(Enter Mattie, a dish in one hand, dish-towel in the other. She stands staring gloomily at her boots.)*

MATTIE

Ych?

FANNIE *(suggestively)*

Ma'am?

MATTIE

Mom.

FANNIE

That's better. Now, will you bring the tea things—quickly!

MATTIE

Yeh—mom! *(She remains standing there, however.)*

FANNIE *(sharply)*

Well? *(Mattie does not answer. Her lower lip sags; her knees bend a little, and the dish, escaping her nerveless fingers, crashes on the floor.)*

FANNIE

Good heavens! What *is* the matter with you? Speak!

MATTIE

(dully, staring at the floor) I ain't sma't.

MRS. PAINTER *(avidly)*

Not smart?

FANNIE

(weakly, tottering a little and putting her hand to her throat) *Not smart?*

MILO

(protesting expansively) Not smart? Dear creature! Oh, you wonderful, simple, primitive creature! Smartness! Pah! *(Turning on the others savagely)* Don't sit there looking at me so—aghast—as if I were uttering heresies. Smart? *We* are *smart*—you—and you —and I. And look at us. *(Turning back to Mattie)* No, no, my dear girl. You are *not* smart, and heaven send you may never come to be smart—you, hiding in your soul something a thousand times more precious than smartness, an element of wisdom—

FANNIE

Milo!

MRS. PAINTER

(almost screaming) It isn't *that,* you fool! It isn't that she means by "not smart." Don't you know what it means down here? Why—it means that one is in a delicate—

MILO

Delicate? You say *"delicate!"* And I say, don't talk to me of delicacy! No, no; look at me as hard as you want to; there's something more priceless in the world than delicacy! We're immersed in it. Yes, I'll say it—immersed—all the vile little soul-stifling inhibitions of soap and tooth-brush, Chinese potteries. I see that I shock you. Well, I am willing to shock you—you, Mrs. Painter, and you, my dear Frances. But I tell you that if this girl here—this splendid, deep-bosomed, ox-eyed earth-woman, is not *delicate,* then as for me—

MRS. PAINTER *(desperately)*

I didn't say *"not delicate!"* I said *in* a delicate—

MILO

(putting his hand to his brow with a sudden new suspicion of light—very weakly) In a delicate —what?

MRS. PAINTER

CONDITION!

MILO

(sitting down abruptly on the couch and staring into vacancy—after a pause—in a wondering whisper) C o n d i t i o n? *(Tableau—Mattie staring at her boots; the two women staring at Milo; Milo staring at nothing. By and by he turns his head, and starts violently as he meets the accusing eyes)* What are you looking at *me* for? *(Seized by a sudden panic, he shakes wild hands at them)* Stop looking at me! Stop it, I say! Stop looking at me! Stop —stop—stop! The—*idea!*

FANNIE

Milo! Oh—Milo—Milo!

MRS. PAINTER

(with a stately sweep to the door) I am afraid

I shall have to say—Good *evening!* *(Exit in a blaze of glory.)*

FANNIE

(with great difficulty—to Mattie) You may leave the room. *(Exit Mattie, her eyes still on the floor. Milo gazes after her, blank and helpless. As the door closes, Fannie sinks on her knees beside the desk, and hiding her face in her hands, shakes with the tumult of her woe, sobbing a muffled "Milo, Milo" from time to time. Milo paces back and forth rapidly.)*

MILO

Frances! Ten minutes ago I would have called the man a liar who told me that you, my wife, had such a *low—suspicious—mind.* Do you hear me? Good God, Fannie! *(Receiving no reply, he subsides on the couch and mops his face. After a moment he resumes in a harassed soliloquy)* The world is full of low minds, I suppose—eternally ready to suspect the worst —licking their lickerish lips for a chance at a man's good name. Pah! *(He groans)* . . . Of course, the girl must be gotten away from here immediately. *Fannie! (Still hearing no answer, he jumps up and moves toward her)* See here! Pull yourself together. There are arrangements to make. This poor creature can't be left here to face the sneers of these damned, narrow-souled provincials. She is, in a sense, a—a—dependent of ours. It seems to me we can't do less than to send her away to some place where she will be looked after— cared for, understood—in the city—*Fanny, will you listen to me? (Grasping her shoulder, not too gently, he tries to uncover her face. She uncovers it herself.)*

FANNIE

(with a suppressed fury) Please don't touch me!

MILO *(snapping)*

Stop it! Stop it, I say!

FANNIE

Don't—touch—me!

MILO

(retreating weakly) But—but I keep telling you—

FANNIE

Please don't keep telling me anything. I can't comprehend anything now. My brain won't work. I think I—I am going crazy. *(She shivers.)*

MILO *(desperately)*

But I tell you—*i t—w a s n' t—M E !*

FANNIE

(her shoulders dropping hopelessly) Denials! Denials! I think I might have been spared *this*.

MILO

But it WASN'T, you know!

FANNIE *(drearily)*

If you must make a brute of yourself, you might have been a gazelle—not a *jackal*. *(Milo stares at her a moment, fascinated; then takes a dazed turn about the room. Somewhere in the circuit he discovers a little spirit of his own.)*

MILO

But if it *had* been, Fannie—

259

FANNIE
(in a sarcastic echo) If it *had* been—

MILO
You wouldn't *mind*, would you?

FANNIE
(shrinking back a step, as before an unfair blow) M-m-mind? *(And then with a terrible gaiety)* Mind? I? Ha-ha-ha-ha—

MILO *(relieved)*
Ah, that's better. That's more like my girl. I knew you wouldn't—even if it—if it—*had* been.

FANNIE
Ha-ha-ha-ha—

MILO
That's right. And now let's think. Have we got a time-table in the house, with connections? And, oh yes, about that address! The what-you-may-call-it Magdalenes' Home. We must get it from Mrs. Painter. The girl mustn't stay here a moment more than is absolutely necessary.

FANNIE
(sitting down) What are you talking about?

MILO
That place in the city. Mrs. Painter thinks well of it.

FANNIE
What has that got to do with it?

MILO *(blankly)*
Why—why—

FANNIE
Of course, the young woman is to remain with us.

MILO

WHAT!

FANNIE *(blandly)*

Naturally. Why, Milo, how queer you talk!
We—you and I—are not going to miss the
fundamental significance of life, are we? We're
not deliberately going to shut the door on life?
We three? This wonderful thing?

MILO *(terribly)*

I must say, my dear girl, this is a poor time for
facetiousness.

FANNIE *(untouched)*

We three! Passing together, hand in hand,
through the unfolding hours of a miracle—

MILO *(ponderously)*

Frances, you are very unkind. You will never
—understand me.

FANNIE

Understand you?

MILO

Not in the deeper sense. You are a woman,
after all. You still cling pathetically to the
grammar-school notion that two and two makes
four.

FANNIE *(unmoved)*

Ah! And that theories are to be put in prac
tice at home?

MILO *(haggardly)*

Theories! My God! Theories! Ideals!
Dreams! Ah, if one could but afford to dream!
(With a heavy wistfulness) But that is for
the angels, and the young. Happy youth, un-
encumbered, foot-free—

FANNIE
All of which is to say—

MILO
Hang take it all. My affairs are in a delicate condition—*(Flinches at the word)* —er—it's a confounded precarious period in my career, my dear girl. Another year, who knows, and I may arrive—*if nothing happens.* After all, we owe a little something to my career.

FANNIE
Ah! Your career!

MILO
And to our own folks—yours and mine. And —and—and to your good—name.

FANNIE
Quite so—my good name. You are beginning to think even of that.

MILO
(in desperation) But I *keep telling you*— *(A loud knock is heard at the outer door. Milo, stepping to the window, cranes out, then, with a look of consternation, runs and sets his back against the door)* It's that Painter woman. What are we going to do?

FANNIE
Do? What should we *do,* when everything is so sweet and natural?

MILO
Fannie, are you *insane?*

FANNIE
No, I am precisely—*sane.* *(Another knock)* Let her in, please.

MILO

(in a pleading whisper) Fannie! Fannie! *(A louder knock.)*

FANNIE *(calling)*

Come in! *(The door opens after a brief struggle; Milo accepts sanctuary in its lee, still visible to the audience, but screened from Mrs. Painter, who enters, and after a suspicious glance at the panels, plops down in a chair and folds her hands.)*

MRS. PAINTER

Well, here I am. I started to go home, and then I just couldn't. When there's anyone in trouble—when there's a chance of anyone's needing help—well, that's the way I am, Mrs. Tate. I said to myself: now, if there's anything I can do—any arrangements I can help them make—to get that wretched girl out of the way before the town is by the ears. Poor Mr. Tate, I said to myself—when all these rough fishermen learn the news—Oh my dear Mrs. Tate, you don't know them! They're ignorant and uncouth, and you wouldn't think they had a spark of sentiment or honor in them; but when anyone gets one of their women-folks in trouble—especially an outsider, like Mr. Tate—well, I said to myself, weak as I am, if there's to be any harm done—any violence—

MILO

(who has been visibly wilting behind the door, bursts forth with an attempt at bravado) Harm? Violence? What do you mean? See here! Do you imagine for one instant that any

man—fisherman or no fisherman—can come around here bulldozing *me*—a perfectly innocent bystander? Have I no protection under the Constitution of this country? *I think I have.* *(Turning on his heel with a hollow majesty, he paces away from them—falters— speaks in a weaker voice)* But I'm forgetting that poor tragic creature. She can't be left here to face the sneering rabble. *(Turning to the others, he speaks in the curt, incisive accents of a man-of-action, a trifle overdone)* I'll get a rig. I'll drive her over to the junction—myself. I'll take her up to the city—myself. I'll make arrangements at the—at the— Mrs. Painter, where was that place?

MRS. PAINTER

(in attitude of deep concentration) Let me think. Let me think.

MILO *(wildly)*

For heaven's sake, don't you remember?

MRS. PAINTER

Let me think, I tell you. Please, please, don't keep hopping about that way or I'll *never* remember. Let me think—was it Ninety-third Street or was it Thirty-ninth Street—or was it Ninety-three some other street—or Thirty-nine—

MILO

But my *dear woman!*

FANNIE

(who has been watching them with an icy scorn —tapping the floor with one foot, but otherwise calm) I think you are both of you mak-

ing rather—rather a spectacle of yourselves. You seem to overlook the fact that all this fuss and flurry is quite unnecessary—quite!

MILO

Unnecessary! *(Dragging out his watch)* Good Lord, woman, look at the time!

MRS. PAINTER

And this was such a good place—not at all like an institution. They have their amusements and things. If a girl *has* to go away—

FANNIE

If she *has* to go away—quite so. I agree with you. But you must remember that this is quite another case, for the girl is *not* going away. She is remaining *here*—quietly—with us.

MILO

(going desperately to pieces) Frances, I swear by—by—I swear if you don't drop that pose and come to your senses—

MRS. PAINTER

(with an air of one remembering—a sudden calmness—a cool, Cheshire smile) Why—of course! *(To Fannie)* Why, my dear, of *course!* *(To Milo)* Oh, Mr. Tate, how stupid of me —knowing your principles! I was—in the excitement and the—ah—danger of the moment —I was just being hopelessly middle-class. Why, *of course!*

MILO

(eyeing them with an elemental ferocity) All right! All right! Seeing that I can hope for no ordinary human assistance from either of you, I—*I wash my hands of you!* Only please

265

keep out of my way! *(Becoming ecstatically busy—dragging a hand-bag from under the couch—hopping about and stuffing into it the most absurd and unrelated objects—draperies, match-safe, etc.)* Please, I say, keep out of my way. *(Looks at watch) Mattie! Mattie!* Where *is* that girl? Good Lord, she'll have no time to pack her things. And—and they might be here any minute!

FANNIE

Who might be here?

MILO

Please don't speak to me. *(Calling)* Mattie! For God's sake, girl, are you deaf? *Mattie! (Enter Mattie.)*

MATTIE

(toward Fannie) Yeh—mom?

MILO

Not *her—me!* Mattie, see here, hurry! Don't keep standing there like a chump. Get your things together—just what you need. Throw them together, girl!

MATTIE *(bewildered)*

(glancing uneasily at Fannie) Huh—mom?

FANNIE

You mustn't take any notice of him, Mattie. He's—

MILO

Frances, oblige me by keeping quiet. *(To Mattie)* Now hurry! You're going away. I'm going to take you to the city. We'll drive to the junction, understand? Junction! Drive!

266

City! Good God, what a bone-head! Going to city! Get that? It's a nice place—not at all like an institution—they have their amusements and things. . . . City! Understand?

MATTIE
(still to Fannie) Huh—mom?

FANNIE
I told you not to pay any attention to him. He's not quite himself. Of course you're *not* going to the city at all. You're going to remain right here with us—right here in the house with us —we three—very quietly—until—until—

MRS. PAINTER
Until your—your—you know—

FANNIE
Is—is—you know—

MRS. PAINTER
—Born.

MILO
Damn it, she *can't!* I say she *can't.* *(To Mattie)* Tell them you *can't!*

MATTIE
No—mom. I can't. My—my old man wouldn't like it, mom.

FANNIE
Your father wouldn't like it?

MATTIE
No—mom. That's right; none of 'em wouldn't like it, mom.

MILO *(aghast)*
Do they—Good God—they don't *know,* do they?

MATTIE

(*sheepishly, eyes on floor*) Yep—mom. I—
told 'em to-day. An' my old man—

MILO

Not another word. For heaven's sake, don't
stand there wasting time! Go! Get a hat on!
What the devil did you have to *tell* them for?
They might be here any minute now—the whole
pack of them. *Hush!* My God, what's that?
(*Grasps Mattie fiercely by shoulder and confronts her accusingly*) GIRL!

MATTIE

I—I guess mebby that's my old man.

MILO (*groans*)

(*then straightens up and looks about him. Steps
hastily to window and peeps out*) No one on
this side—yet.

MATTIE

(*to Fannie*) Should I leave 'im in, mom?

MILO

(*darting toward her and grasping her roughly
by the wrist*) You fool! Come! We'll make
a run for it the front way. Come along, I say!
(*Starts to drag her by main force toward the
front door. Mattie, aroused from her native
coma by his violence and the savage expression
on his face, struggles frantically, appealing to
Fannie.*)

MATTIE

Oh, no, mom—no, mom—no, mom— (*As
Milo, dragging her, puts out his hand to open
the front door, terror overcomes her and she
begins to shriek incoherently. From off-stage—*

kitchen-way—comes the sound of a door broken in and deep masculine rumblings. Enter Mr. Snow, a Fisherman, disheveled, wild-eyed, carrying a trawl-tub and armed with a gaff. At sight of tableau by door he draws up in the dramatic attitude of a tiger about to spring.)

SNOW

Leave be with your hands there!

MILO

(letting Mattie go and sinking back against the wall, staring with an appealing fascination at the intrduer—weakly) It wasn't me—I swear —I give you my word—it wasn't me.

SNOW

Wasn't *you?* You stand there and tell me it wasn't you? And me seeing you with my very eyes? Wasn't you, eh? Mattie, come here! *(Mattie runs and takes exhausted shelter beside him.)*

MILO *(chattering)*

It *wasn't* me. It wasn't—it wasn't. Honestly, Mr.—Mr.—

SNOW

Stow it. I seen you; so stow it before I heave this tub at your head. I don't care who you are; I know what you done; I seen you doing it, and I'm going to give you a lesson to chaw on— I'll be dumned if I ain't. *(Advances menacingly.)*

MILO *(screeching)*

I didn't! Don't you touch an innocent man. It was someone else did it—I swear by my honor. Somebody else did it!

SNOW

(showing first signs of puzzlement) Somebody else done—*what?*

MILO

IT!

SNOW

It—*what?*

MRS. PAINTER

He means—got her in—in—trouble.

SNOW

In *trouble! Her? HIM? SAY!*

FANNIE

(breathlessly—plucking at her skirts) You didn't know?

MRS. PAINTER

—That your daughter was—

SNOW

My *daughter?*

FANNIE

But she said you were—

MRS. PAINTER

—You were her—old man.

SNOW

Old man? Of course I'm her old man. And she's my old woman.

FANNIE

Do you mean she is your—

MRS. PAINTER

—Your—your—

MILO

(uncovering, dazed — transfigured eyes) — Wife?

SNOW

Well, for Cripe's sake now—what did you think?

MILO

(*tottering to couch and sinking down*) We— we simply didn't—think.

FANNIE

We didn't know she was—

MRS. PAINTER

Married.

FANNIE

We all want to beg a thousand pardons, Mr.— Mr.—

MILO

(*weakly—mopping his brow*) Ten thousand! Ten thousand!

SNOW

Well, I don't know. Don't seem to understand. But I just come up here to tell you I thought best the woman should quit work now. She ain't smart, you know—

MILO

Yes, yes; that's all right. We understand, old chap. Yes, indeed. Good—good-bye.

SNOW

Good-day to you all. . . . Tell 'em good-day, Mattie, girl.

MATTIE

Good-day to you—mom. (*Exeunt—somehow or other. For a time deep silence reigns. Milo, relapsed on the couch, veils his face with a handkerchief. Mrs. Painter sits down in a chair*

271

very quietly, takes her cheeks between her hands, and stares at nothing. After a moment Milo summons strength to arise and stand mid-stage in an attitude convenient for his wife to cast her arms about him.)

FANNIE

Milo! Milo! I've been such a mean, shallow little ninny. Oh, I can never, never, never forgive myself.

MRS. PAINTER

(to vacancy) I wonder—I wonder—

FANNIE

Milo, Milo darling, look at me. I'll never doubt you again as long as I live.

MRS. PAINTER

I remember now; it was 39 East Ninety—

[CURTAIN]

4-2603